Say What?

A Fresh Look at the Great Stories of Jesus

Ted Creen

This book is dedicated to my parents, Agnes and Norman Creen, who are now with the Lord. I feel privileged to have grown up in such a loving and caring home. They were always supportive of my creative endeavours and would be proud of this book.

I also dedicate this book to my wife Lorraine, who was part of the development of this book as we shared together in ministry at Huron Feathers, Sauble Beach and whose prayers I have always valued throughout my years of ministry.

SAY WHAT?
Copyright © 2018 by Ted Creen

Scriptures are taken from the Good News Translation–Second Edition © 1992 by American Bible Society. Used by permission.

Printed in Canada

ISBN: 978-1-4866-1680-0

Word Alive Press
119 De Baets Street, Winnipeg, MB R2J 3R9
www.wordalivepress.ca

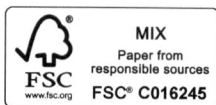

WORD ALIVE
—P R E S S—

FSC
www.fsc.org

MIX
Paper from
responsible sources
FSC® C016245

Cataloguing in Publication may be obtained through Library and Archives Canada

Acknowledgements

This book began with a series of messages prepared for the summer of 2017 at Huron Feathers Presbyterian Centre at Sauble Beach, Ontario. Huron Feathers is a unique and highly creative summer ministry to a resort community located on a long stretch of beautiful sandy beach on Lake Huron. Ministry is offered to all ages: Sunday worship, day camp, youth programs, and many special events.

A dedicated group of people from that summer congregation joined my wife Lorraine and me on Wednesday mornings to discuss the parables of Jesus. We dug into those texts and discussed their implications for our faith and life today. Ideas and comments shared in those meetings have been added to flesh out the original messages in preparation for this book.

At the final meeting of the group, one member challenged me to transform our summer's study into a book. I acknowledge the support and input from these friends in faith at Huron Feathers.

I also want to thank my wife Lorraine and my daughter Sarah for reviewing the manuscript and providing helpful suggestions.

Here is the book!

Contents

Images and Stories

Chapter One

OF THE MANY ASPECTS OF MINISTRY I HAVE BEEN BLESSED TO SHARE OVER many years, I feel a special calling to preaching. I enjoy the study and preparation in order to impact the lives of my congregations with the Word of God. I embrace the challenge to bring that truth into their current lives and the world in which we live.

At times I have experienced some humbling moments as well, times when people have remarked positively not about my carefully crafted sermon but about the object lesson I used with the children that day. I admit I enjoy those times as well, seeking out some object or image that will grab the attention of very young children. I've come to realize that there have been times, perhaps many, when those children didn't quite get the connection I was attempting to make between the object and the biblical truth, but adults did. I know now that they pay close attention to those children's times in the service, often remembering the object lesson more easily than my sermons.

"Wasn't that great what the pastor shared with the children this morning?" someone might say.

I call such reactions, when the truth of an object lesson is absorbed by our minds, a "say what" moment.

Following a recent interdenominational service, as I was enjoying meeting and greeting friends from the various churches in the community, one of those friends sought me out to share a story with me. He wanted to make sure that it was okay with me for him to have used an image I had developed in a workshop he had attended. The workshop had dealt with the grieving process. Simply put, I had brought a large jagged rock to illustrate the pain associated with the loss of a close loved one. We carry that rock, and the jagged edges often bruise us in the early stages of grief. I then brought out a smaller, smoother rock. I used that stone to illustrate that although the rock of grief never leaves, by going through the grieving process it can be smoothed down.

My friend had shared this object lesson with others. He had found it to be very helpful for himself and others, and I assured him that he was free to use it as often as he could.

I have come to grasp what Jesus obviously knew well. He would take a common, everyday object and then use it to apply an eternal truth. Such was Jesus's dynamic storytelling ability. The word we use for this technique of placing an object alongside an essential teaching is *parable*. It comes from *para*, meaning "alongside of."

Whether it was a seed to be sown, a bit of leaven for baking, a coin lost on the floor, or a lamp put under a bushel, Jesus was an artist of words. He caught the attention of his listeners with a number of these examples. Those who heard these object lessons went home impacted by the simplicity of the truth that was now fixed in their minds.

Those images stay with us as well. So it's not surprising that so many of us can recall object lessons or images in a worship service more than the numerous points of a sermon. We will consider a number of those images used by Jesus in his teaching ministry throughout this book.

My wife and I visited some friends of ours a while back. We enjoyed a great meal and time visiting and playing with their children. As the time grew late, bedtime beckoned the children. One bedtime ritual for many families, certainly the one we were visiting, is to read a story prior to being tucked in.

I wanted in on the action, so with a five-year-old girl I launched into an imagination story that popped into my head.

"Once upon a time long ago, three bunnies lived in a deep green forest. You might say they all looked the same, but if you looked closely, each of them had a special appearance. White Paws, of course, had beautiful white feet which everyone admired. Midnight had the darkest fur you ever saw on a bunny, and he was really proud of how he looked. The third bunny was called One Ear…"

That was as far as I got, since it was late and bedtime beckoned.

I realized one crucial lesson as that little girl was trundled up the stairs by her grandmother: once a story is begun, you are drawn into the narrative and it's hard to let it go. We want to know just how it turns out, even sometimes flipping to the final chapter of a novel.

"I'm sure he knows how the story ends," this little girl called out as she was led upstairs.

But actually, I didn't know. I had begun a story, created some interesting characters, but I didn't have any idea of the ending—not at that point.

I realized that I had a task ahead of me. I would go back to the hotel, pull out my laptop, and finish the story so that this little girl would have the full story with an ending the next morning when she woke up.

In case I have roused your curiosity about how I ended this story, I will include the whole thing in the appendix at the end of this book.

Again, Jesus was an artist with words. He created these stories, *parables*, from his deep observations of the life going on all around him. Parables have been called "earthly stories with heavenly meanings." Jesus lay profound spiritual truths alongside his stories, and when Jesus began a story, his listeners—and us, reading them today—were drawn in, discovering the setting and meeting the characters.

We cannot let a story go until we know how it ends.

With this simple technique, Jesus, once he had the full attention of his listeners, inserted a dramatic twist, an unexpected "say what" moment that fully reinforced the spiritual truth he was teaching. It is those moments I want to recapture in this book.

Here are some points to remember as we consider a number of those dynamic parables of Jesus:

- Jesus was a keen observer, drawing on everyday life for his images and stories. Those hearing him could easily identify with both the situation and characters of his parables.

They may not have happened exactly as Jesus told them, but they easily could have happened. We, too, can identify with those situations and characters.

- In order for us to receive our "say what" moment with the stories and images of Jesus's teaching ministry, we need to recover the context of those parables, the everyday culture of Jewish life two thousand years ago. Then we will be able to grasp the significance of the point Jesus was drawing out.

- It will be important to keep our minds on the essential spiritual truths Jesus was leading us towards and not get bogged down in details of the story or make too much of them. We have a tendency to interpret the parables of Jesus as allegories—that is, to try to place a spiritual identity on each character and every detail. Rather, we should remember that the strength of a parable is the central point that Jesus wanted to drive home.

- As we will discover, Jesus's parables were often spoken in tense situations or to answer difficult questions. Jesus could use these parables to convey deep truths that otherwise might not have been tolerated by the original listeners. Remember this story technique: we are drawn into the story, listening carefully, until Jesus pulls off a dramatic twist. We then discover that we have opened ourselves to the lesson Jesus was driving home.

- These object lessons and stories of Jesus demand a response from his listeners, even today. Stories elicit thoughts, feelings, emotions, and responses. When we consider even very familiar parables of Jesus, we should be open to our own responses.

With this background in place, let us consider a number of the images and stories of Jesus. With each chapter, I want to develop certain contexts in the following ways.

I'll begin with some "say what" moments from my own life, a few modern parables and stories triggered by certain words we use. I do this to position ourselves with those who were hearing the words of Jesus for the first time. To fully grasp the "say what" moments in Jesus's teachings we must consider to whom the words were directed. In doing that, we will discover that we have much in common with the folks hanging on to the images and stories of Jesus. Our humanity mirrors theirs, and the issues Jesus was addressing with his stories more often than not are relevant to issues in our own lives today.

Next we'll dig into the images and stories, recovering the culture behind them to arrive at the point Jesus was making, allowing it to ring out loud and clear. With each image or story, we need to carefully consider the trigger that caused Jesus to teach about it. He often employed stories to respond to questions and issues brought forward by those around him. Understanding the context of Jesus's images and stories will enable us to more fully appreciate the people's original responses.

Finally, I will return to the essential point Jesus was making and pose some leading questions as you apply the truths to your own life. I want to encourage you to experience your own reactions.

I will conclude each chapter with a prayer to direct your further meditation.

Entitlement
and
Resentment

Chapter Two

POWERFUL EMOTIONS OFTEN RISE UP WITHIN ME AND CATCH ME OFF-GUARD. One emotion is based upon what seems to be a basic human drive: that life should be *fair*. I think this began when I was little. Did I get proper treatment or did someone else receive a larger share of attention? Was I given a just reward for my good behaviour or did someone else get away with bad behaviour while I was striving to do my best? Did they get ahead because of what they did? Every child cries out, sometimes often, "But it's just not fair!"

Where did this come from? Partially, such feelings arise from our innate sense of justice, which is good. What's problematic is that such feelings can develop into a sense of *entitlement*: "I've been good, therefore God should reward me. I feel entitled to my reward and upset when I judge that someone else has received more than me. I feel there should be a higher reward for sacrificial service."

How do I become aware of such feelings of entitlement? The answer: when I discover the sharp pain of *resentment* where it shouldn't exist. Check yourself. When have you felt the stab of resentment in your life? What triggered it? Who brought it out of the deep places inside you? How did you react?

We are still that child: "But it's just not fair!" Do you discover a stab of resentment about someone who receives the promotion you felt was yours? When someone else in your profession earns far more than you? When you walk past the grand mansion on the next street and must return home to deal with your leaky plumbing? When someone in your family commands more than their share of attention?

Ponder these feelings as we consider a parable with a powerful "say what" moment.

THE LABOURERS IN THE VINEYARD
READ MATTHEW 20:1-16

Before we dig into this story, go back and read Matthew 19:16–30. A rich young man came to Jesus asking about what he must do to receive salvation. Jesus responded by directing the young man back to the covenant commandments the individual thought he had observed all his life: love God and love your neighbour.

In a surprising turn, Jesus then instructed that young man to sell everything he had, give those resources to the poor, and return to follow Jesus as a disciple. The young man sadly turned away, unable and unwilling to part with his wealth.

This raised questions among the disciples, particularly Peter. Turning to Jesus, he asked, *"Look... we have left everything and followed you. What will we have?"* (Matthew 19:27)

Basically, Peter was experiencing that feeling of entitlement rising up. If the rich young man couldn't find it in his heart to give up everything to follow Jesus, does it not follow that the disciples, who had given up occupation and home to follow Jesus, should be well rewarded for their effort? Peter was reassured that there would be a future reward for their service, but Jesus was aware that his disciples required a basic lesson in the radical grace of the kingdom of God.

Jesus began to tell a story based on a landowner who required his labourers to bring in the harvest from his vineyard. Commentator William Barclay has pointed out that this parable is based on the reality of the grape harvest:

The grape harvest ripened towards the end of September, and then close on its heels the rains came. If the harvest was not in-gathered before the rains broke, then it was ruined;

and so to get the harvest in was a frantic race against time. Any worker was welcome, even if he could give only an hour to the work.[1]

Barclay goes on to describe the "labour exchange" of that day: potential workers would gather in the marketplace and potential employers would come to hire workers for the day. Work was necessary for survival, so it wouldn't have been unusual for workers to wait all day for a chance at earning some money.

All is usual up to this point in the story. Then comes the "say what" moment.

At the end of the day, the owner of the vineyard issued payment to the labourers. Some had worked all day, some a half day, others only the final hour. However, all workers were paid *the same amount.* Say what? That certainly was the response of those who had toiled all day under the hot sun. They grumbled and complained, resentful of those who had worked for far less time yet earned the same amount. "But it's not fair," they said, feeling entitled to much more.

Yet they had agreed to what they were paid. If no one else had been hired, they would have been satisfied. The problem arose when they felt slighted and resentful of others.

At first sight, it would appear that they had a point. Our sense of justice recoils at the thought of someone doing far less work but earning the same pay. Do you recognize this feeling of resentment? How often have you felt slighted at the comparison you've made between yourself and someone else?

We need to consider the response of the owner of the vineyard: *"Don't I have the right to do as I wish with my own money? Or are you jealous because I am generous?"* (Matthew 20:15)

Remember that a parable is a story with an essential point. Jesus wasn't advocating labour injustice. He was responding to a question about who should be rewarded and how we should be rewarded in his kingdom. We must embrace divine justice, which is based on mercy and grace,

---

1 William Barclay, *The Daily Study Bible: The Gospel of Matthew, Volume 2* (Burlington, ON: G.R. Welch Co., 1975), 222.

to offset the feelings of entitlement and resentment that can overpower us. In another parable, we'll meet a joyless elder brother who, despite his diligence and hard work, nursed feelings of entitlement and resentment.

Simply put, the lesson in Matthew 20:1–16 is another example of Jesus's proclamation of radical grace. It's an invitation to the kingdom. Some will respond early, some after struggling with life issues, and still others with a deathbed repentance. Even the criminal hanging on the cross next to Jesus was rewarded with paradise. All are eagerly sought by Jesus and all will be welcomed when they allow Jesus to become Lord of their lives.

The reward of eternal life is the same for all. This is truly the good news of the gospel. Like the owner of the vineyard, God is good and his heart is one of compassion. The essential truth of Jesus's teaching is that God's gift of forgiving love and abundant living is a *gift*, not a *reward*, and it is God's to freely give to those who will receive. Grace cannot be earned, only accepted. That surely is good news, as no one is truly deserving of such love, even if they may feel entitled.

The radical point of this story is simple: grace, salvation, abundant life, joy, peace, and all the benefits of the kingdom of God in Christ are to be considered a gift.

Remember the initial context of this parable: Peter's question about what he and the other disciples will get out of their sacrificial service. Since grace is a gift, it should be received in joy. Such joy will create a loving response to the Giver. This means that everything we do in the name of Jesus is not to be calculated but enjoyed. We go to work in God's world as a response to God's loving provision for us, whether it be early in life or at the end.

With the right attitude, every day of serving Jesus is a reward in itself. Each day we can begin by saying, "This is the day that the Lord has made. I will rejoice and be glad in it." Every opportunity to reach out to another person with the love and grace of Jesus is a bonus. We rejoice with everyone who joins us in this wonderful experience of receiving Jesus as Lord and Saviour, no matter at which point in their lives they make that choice. This is the antidote to entitlement and its companion, resentment.

Living Out Our "Say What" Moment

At what point in your life did you agree to be part of the kingdom of God in Jesus? What has being a worker in God's vineyard been like for you? Express thanks for the time you have been able to spend sharing in the building of this kingdom.

You have been given the joy of participating with Jesus in building a kingdom of ultimate love. If you feel that you are working too hard for too little, remember the parable of the sheep and the goats (Matthew 25:31–46), which we will explore later in the book. It is in acts of sacrificial service that we meet the living Jesus. It must be a joy, not a drudgery. Rather than waiting for payment at the end of the day, we can experience joy in serving Jesus every minute of the day! We are constantly rewarded with the flowing of his love into us as we flow that love outwards in a continual cycle.

Have feelings of entitlement and resentment ever caused you to miss out on the full experience of serving in the kingdom of God? Have you ever complained about all the work you have to do, the expectations others have of you, that there aren't enough other workers to help you out? Consider new areas in which you may experience the joy of serving Jesus in his kingdom. Are there new ways you can employ the gifts and abilities God has graced you with? Who can you invite to become partners in this wonderful kingdom of grace, with whom you can share the joy of serving Jesus? Are you able to rejoice with those who have received and accepted the invitation from Jesus to join in his kingdom?

A Prayer for Our "Say What" Life

Loving God, you have called me into your kingdom. I am loved, forgiven, and empowered to serve you with all the gifts and abilities you have created in me. I realize that I have complained about this at times. What I do often seems to be taken for granted. Others receive more recognition. There are times when I feel tired and discouraged.

Remind me again that serving Jesus is my loving response for his calling me. Restore to me the joy of doing even the simplest tasks to build up your kingdom. May I always keep in mind that I am serving you, not earning the praise of others. Knowing this, may I not hesitate to give praise and thanks to those others who serve faithfully around me so that together we can share the excitement of working together for you. Give me opportunities to invite others to share in the life of your kingdom. In Jesus's name, amen.

Value

Chapter Three

A MOVIE I OFTEN ENJOY WATCHING, PARTICULARLY AROUND CHRISTMAS, IS the 1946 Frank Capra classic *It's a Wonderful Life*. Jimmy Stewart plays George Bailey, who has experienced some disappointments in life. His ambition to travel is cut short by the death of his father, causing George to take over the family Building and Loan business. His honeymoon is cut short when George has to bail out the business with the money he had saved up for the trip.

On Christmas Eve 1945, George finds himself at the end of his rope. His Uncle Billy has lost a bank deposit of $8,000, which actually was scooped up by the unscrupulous Mr. Potter, who wants to take total control of the town of Bedford Falls. Facing disaster, not to mention the sheriff, George plans to jump to his death into a freezing river. However, an aspiring angel, Clarence, is sent to prevent George from taking his life.

Clarence, having prevented George from drowning, still faces the challenge of lifting George out of a deep depression. Mr. Potter had earlier taunted George with his failures, saying that all George had was a $500 insurance policy and that he was worth more dead than alive. George agreed that it would have been better if he hadn't been born at all.

Hearing this, the plot unfolds. Angel Clarence enables George to experience the negative consequences to his family and community if he hadn't been born, from the loss of housing for many low-income families to the death of his brother due to a tragic accident. He discovers that the entire town in which he lives has benefited from his life and deeds in many ways, and without him their lives would be very bleak indeed.

I find this plot twist intriguing. What if I had never been born? What would the world be like? What would be missing? When I'm frustrated with life's circumstances, or wishing that things had turned out better, this is a good corrective: consider what just one "wonderful life" has provided to the world. No matter what disappointments or setbacks a person experiences, their life is one of great value.

God's creation of you is unique and special. You are one of a kind, never to be duplicated. Our task in life is to discover and live out that God-created potential, to make a significant difference where God has placed us.

Are you willing to embrace the great worth of your life in the eyes of God? Are voices from the past suggesting that you're not talented enough, good-looking enough, smart enough, or popular enough? Silence them with the value that our loving God holds for you through his Word. Are you secure enough to withstand our culture's demand for appearance and visible success in wealth or status?

Consider also the worth or value you place on others. Can you see them through the eyes of our loving God? This is very much a contemporary issue. Today, we see far too many cases of bullying, of putting people down for their appearance, of attempting to build up one's ego at the expense of another. How comfortable are you in the presence of someone very different from you? Are there people or groups that you simply avoid? Do you go out of your way to warmly greet someone new and different at church, or do you only fellowship with friends you know well? How well do you demonstrate the value of every single person you meet each day?

Let us consider some parables which describe the value God has for each one of us.

THE LOST AND FOUND PARABLES
READ LUKE 15:1-24

Before we get into these three stories, take note again of the context that prompted Jesus to tell them. One day, a number of tax collectors and outcasts gathered to listen to Jesus. That was a common experience, as these people were drawn by Jesus's loving compassion. Just as common, others were hanging around the edges of the crowd: scribes and Pharisees. As was often the case, these religious officials didn't take kindly to the scruffy crowd gathered around Jesus. They were particularly offended that he shared meals with them. They started grumbling, considering such a crowd to be filled with unclean and spiritually iffy folks.

Note that the Pharisees devoted their lives to following the letter of the Mosaic Law. That observance took a lot of effort, for there were a myriad of detailed regulations for them to follow in order to achieve righteousness. These religious officials reacted so often to the ministry of Jesus because of their rules and regulations.

William Barclay gives a helpful background:

> It was an offence to the Scribes and Pharisees that Jesus companied with men and women who, by the orthodox, were labelled as sinners. The Pharisees gave to people who did not keep the law a general classification. They called them *The People of the Land*. There was a complete barrier between the Pharisees and the People of the Land… a Pharisee was forbidden to be the guest of any such man, or to have him as his guest. He was even forbidden so far as it was possible, to have any business dealings with him, or to buy anything from him of sell anything to him. It was the deliberate Pharisaic aim to avoid every contact with the People of the Land… obviously, they would be shocked to the core at the way in which Jesus companied with people who were not only rank outsiders, but sinners, contact with whom would necessarily defile.[2]

In these parables, Jesus presents us with a very different set of values on human life. For religious officials, value was dependent on their observance of the law. For Jesus, value was intrinsic to each human being. Each one of us is a beloved child of the Creator God.

---

2   William Barclay, *The Daily Study Bible: The Gospel of Luke* (Edinburgh, UK: Saint Andrew Press, 1972), 206.

To push those hearing these parables to a "say what" moment, Jesus used the "lost and found" example. He presents three stories of something or someone lost and the joy of them being sought out and found. Let us explore each of the stories, giving note to the various ways in which we can become lost.

The Lost Sheep

Sheep generally don't seek to leave the flock; they often just wander off. Nibbling a bit of grass here, then there, they perhaps fall into a ravine or end up on a path far from safety.

In this story, the shepherd is responsible for looking after a flock of one hundred sheep, but one sheep has gone astray. A reasoned approach might be to let that sheep go and concentrate on the ninety-nine that are safe. In this story, however, the vagrant sheep is just as valuable as any of the others—so much so that the shepherd leaves the many to seek out and recover the lost one.

We can become lost by drifting away, sometimes without realizing it until we find ourselves down a ravine of life. Minister Ray Stedman has pointed out that the lost sheep

> represents people who are lost, but who never intended to be lost. They never meant to be, and they don't know how it happened. In complete sincerity of purpose they suddenly find themselves lost, and they do not know how it came about…
>
> This is the picture our Lord gives us of certain people who are intent only on the present experience. They are living just for the moment. They do not intend to get lost; they do not intend to waste their lives.[3]

---

3   Ray Stedman, "God and the Unthinking." May 25, 1969 (https://www.raystedman. org/thematic-studies/treasures-of-the-parables/god-and-the-unthinking).

The Lost Coin

In this case, the valuable coin didn't get lost through its own fault but because of the fault of a woman who had carelessly let it slip through her fingers. This coin was a Greek *drachma*, a silver coin, the common wage for a day's labour. It's also quite possible that the coin in this story was a special ornament, a *semedi*. It was customary for married Jewish women to wear a headdress of ten such coins, very much like a wedding band today.

This parable is a reminder that even though we are of great value to God, circumstances of life, other people, and sudden changes beyond our control can push us away from God's love into feelings of loneliness and worthlessness. However the coin was lost, it remained of great value to the woman of the house who spared no effort in finding it, sweeping the place clean until it was restored to its rightful place.

The Lost Son

In this dramatic story of a father with two sons, the younger brother demonstrated his sense of being lost through a deliberate act of will. He demanded that his father immediately grant him his share of his inheritance, one-third of the father's estate, with the elder brother receiving the larger amount. The younger son wasn't content to wait until his father's death to claim his share; he wanted it all now! He was, in effect, declaring that his father might as well be dead. He had decided to forsake the family home and seek his life somewhere, perhaps anywhere, else.

The young man was cashing in and leaving home forever. If he was going to be lost, he would be truly lost and, in his mind, have a great time doing it.

After a time of living it up in a far country, the young man wasted away his inheritance and was left in a bad state, starving and feeding swine to stay alive. Eventually he came to his senses, realizing that the servants back home were better off than he was. Maybe it was time to return home, he thought, even if it was to live as a servant. At least he would have food to satisfy his craving belly.

Yet when he returned, his father rushed out to greet the returning "prodigal," brushing aside the young man's carefully prepared speech of contrition and ordering regal clothing and calling for a banquet to be prepared.

A lost sheep or a lost coin would have interested those scribes and Pharisees, but this scoundrel of a son crawling back home and being greeted with so much gusto by his father certainly would have evoked a strong, "Say what?"

After what the son had done to his father, many would have expected the father to respond with "I have no son!" rather than lavish forgiveness. Even if the son begged for mercy, it would have been acceptable for the father to refuse to consider the request. For the religious officials, the image of the father, gathering up his robe and *running out* to greet the wayward son, would have been scandalous. The boy had brought this on himself. There had to be some consequences to pay back some of what had been wasted.

Yet here was Jesus, offering a great "say what" moment of the loving heart of God. No matter how we might become lost, whether by wandering off, falling prey to life's circumstances, or making foolish and wrong decisions, Father God yearns for the restoration of relationship with us. Grace means no matter what! And there is to be great rejoicing when restoration takes place and the lost is found.

Living Out Our "Say What" Moment

Have you ever thought about what the world would be like if you hadn't been born? Take some time to consider it and savour the blessings that God has brought into the world through you. Give thanks!

Have you experienced being lost in relation to the love of Jesus? Have you allowed your life to wander away like a wayward sheep? Have you let the cares and concerns of life or the pressures of contemporary culture draw you away from your relationship with God? Can you picture Jesus, the loving shepherd, coming to bring you back to his place of love and life?

Do you identify with the lost coin? Have the circumstances of life driven you from the place of love to the floor of despair and depression? Has illness, poverty, loss, or frustration disabled your faith? Can you picture a God who, like the woman in the story, will spare no effort to find you where you are and joyfully restore you to a place of living relationship with him?

Finally, maybe there are some of you who, due to some very bad decisions and actions, have pushed yourself far from your father's house. Perhaps you feel a deep sense of shame and failure, even fear that God will judge you severely. Others may have judged you as lost. Now picture the father in the parable, constantly looking down the road for his son and then joyfully rushing out to embrace him. Picture God doing the very same for you!

In all these parables, we see the wonderful image of a loving, grace-filled God who desires a deep, living relationship with his children. God seeks to restore these damaged relationships and will go to any length to make that happen. God will not judge; he will hold out forgiveness and restoration.

On the other hand, think about those religious officials in the crowd. Resist the temptation of writing off these scribes and Pharisees as being self-righteous bigots. There was a reason Jesus often sparred with them, as we will discover with later parables. Jesus had a love for the covenant relationship of his Jewish heritage and he was saddened that manmade traditions had saddled the faith. His first task was not to dismantle the current religion but to bring its heart back, to call the faithful to a living relationship with a living God. Jesus cared deeply for those who carried the responsibility for worship and faith.

With that in mind, we may find some similarity between ourselves and those religious officials. Due to their rules and regulations, they were deeply troubled over the fact that Jesus would associate and share meals with people who were considered unclean and sinful. They looked down upon them—especially as we will discover in the parable of the Pharisee and the Publican—with a smug sense of superiority. Have you ever felt spiritual superiority welling up inside you? Has that ever blocked you from reaching out to a wayward child of God in your life or community?

There is a bit of Pharisee in all of us, and it would do us good to consider parables like these to challenge some hidden assumptions in our lives. We are to be Christ-like. Entering into the power of these parables and walking the pathways with Jesus in the gospels will constantly bring us face to face with individuals that society has pushed to the edges.

How did Jesus continually reach out to those broken by life? The answer lies in these parables. Jesus had the heart of a loving, compassionate, forgiving God, like the father rushing out to embrace the wayward son. Jesus sees each individual not as a sinner or a prostitute or a scoundrel tax collector but as a precious child of God worth redeeming.

We must do the same. Walk your streets, and with everyone you see think, "There is a precious child God has created and for whom he deeply cares." No matter what you feel about that person, simply pray love for them, and if possible reach out to encourage them. Say what? It will make a remarkable difference.

A Prayer for Living Out Our "Say What" Moment

Lord God, we are thankful for your constant love for us. No matter where we've been or what we've done, you yearn for a deep and lasting relationship with us. I confess that there have been times when the cares and voices of the world have drawn me away from enjoying fellowship with you. At times, my carelessness toward my spiritual life has come between us. At times, harsh circumstances have drawn me too far into my own misery and away from you. And yes, at times my poor decisions and choices have separated me from your love. Yet like the loving father in the parable, you are always looking out for me.

Lord, let me return to you as you run out to embrace me in your grace. May I model that same love for someone who feels lost in life. Lord, lead me to truly see in each face the precious child you have created in them. May I never be so offended or put off by their circumstance that I fail to reach out in love. May all our churches become places of refuge and healing for those broken by the strains of life. May we truly revel in celebrations of joy as we discover what has been lost and welcome God's returning children. In Jesus's name I pray, amen.

Limitations

Chapter Four

HAVE YOU EVER EXPERIENCED AN ATTACK OF THE YABBUTS? I CERTAINLY have. What is a yabbut? The attack comes when you begin to dream about a new possibility or when an opportunity suddenly presents itself. You begin to imagine what life might be like if you followed that lead into a new experience or made a decision that would really change your life. Such dreaming, I have discovered, seems to be immediately followed by another act of human imagination: fears and doubts.

Almost in answer to those opportunities and possibilities, our minds counter them with the "yes but." The new possibility does seem positive and wonderful, *but...* and our minds churn out all sorts of doubts and fears.

These yabbuts may arise from our past: old voices we've harboured deep inside our hearts that shout, "You're not talented enough, tough enough, or smart enough to take on this new opportunity." Perhaps you're carrying around the weight of former failures: "Well, I tried something new and radical in the past and look what happened."

What about you? What yabbuts have you entertained in your life?

Yabbuts are intense limitations we place on ourselves, and they can become serious obstacles to us truly living full lives. Check out John 10:10, one of the key scriptures that my wife and I meditate upon. Jesus announces there that he desires to give us a "full and abundant life." To me, that means a life of overcoming doubts, fears, and those nasty yabbuts.

However, in that same verse Jesus describes an enemy who comes to "steal, kill, and destroy."

The entire chapter of John 10 is devoted to the wonderful image of sheep and shepherds. Sheep in those days spent the nights in the safety of a common sheepfold. Each morning, the shepherd would call out the sheep of his own flock, and they would recognize his voice. He would lead them to the green pastures and still waters of the surrounding hillsides. Then it would be back to the sheep-fold in the evening, where a shepherd would guard the entrance to the fold from all predators or robbers. He would literally lay down his life for those sheep. An enemy would have to climb the walls of the sheepfold to get to the sheep.

We have enemies—that's the underlying truth—and one of the attacks of our enemy, satan, can come from inside us: from our minds, wills, and emotions. The yabbuts that attack the abundance of our lives, driving us away from our dreams and opportunities, are one such attack. The fears that enable the enemy to sap our strength and drain our joy are another. The unnecessary limitations we place upon our lives, robbing us of fully embracing all that life has for us, is yet a third kind of attack.

Consider the times when you've confronted a yabbut attack and broken through it to make a significant decision or embrace a life-affirming possibility. In an earlier book, *Get a Life!*, I wrote about a trip I took to Peru. I reflected on the opportunities we often have to fulfill a dream, ambition, or challenge. The two times I visited Peru were all about fulfilling dreams and taking on challenges, since both times I hiked the Inca Trail to the legendary lost city of Machu Picchu. The trips were full of challenge and adventure. I savoured the beauty of the Andes Mountains, but hiking through them meant dealing with high altitude. At one point, I had to climb up to a pass fourteen thousand feet above sea level. It didn't help that the pass was named "Dead Woman's Pass"—although that name referred to the shape of the mountain, not what had happened to earlier trekkers!

Meeting the challenges, embracing the history and culture, and taking in the vistas made for a magnificent experience. My first time hiking the Inca Trail was with a friend, and during that trip we even celebrated my birthday. The porters were able to come up with a birthday cake they cooked on a stove they carried with them.

I had so many stories and photos from that trip to share with everyone. Hearing my exploits challenged my daughter Sarah to start dreaming of hiking with me. It was wonderful to share with her my second journey along the Inca Trail, where we had still more adventures and the challenge of that high pass with very thin oxygen.

I'm reflecting on those adventures now because I could have just left them in the bin of unfulfilled dreams. I have other adventures I'd love to tackle, but at this point they remain on the backburner. Preparing for my trips to Peru demanded that I get myself in good physical shape, acquire passports and permits, and get some inoculations. At various points, I remember thinking, "Well, perhaps I'm not going to be in good enough shape for this trek" or "Perhaps I should think of something a little less demanding." These sorts of thoughts place limitations on us that hinder our ability to truly get out and experience life. These yabbuts need to be challenged and conquered.

Let us return to the parable Jesus told of a father and his two sons, but this time consider the elder brother's self-imposed limitations to live a full life. There's a party going on, and the father desires his elder son to come and join the fun and festivities. But the elder brother is full of yabbuts!

THE ELDER BROTHER
READ LUKE 15:25-32

We dealt with the return of the younger son in the last chapter. Too often, we place all the emphasis on the wayward son, but there's much, much more to this parable, particularly when Jesus presents the reaction of the elder son to his brother's return.

The scribes and Pharisees would have reacted with astonishment to the extravagance of the father's embrace of his returning youngest son. They would have expected instead a full repentance; the father should have insisted on some restitution. After all, that prodigal son had frittered away one-third of the family's value. At the extreme, those religious authorities wouldn't have questioned the father for simply accepting the younger son's prepared speech and allowing him to simply become one of the estate's hired servants—but not a son, not with a robe, ring, and party.

With the banquet getting underway and the band tuning up and guests arriving, we meet the elder brother. He's working his heart out for the family farm, just as he had for all those years while the younger brother was living it up. Duty, responsibility, and effort were the keystones of the elder brother's life. Should those not be recognized and affirmed? Those values were prized by the Pharisees in their total obedience and adherence to the Mosaic Law.

However, when the brother heard the sounds of a party getting started back in the family home, he wasn't happy about it. He was deeply offended. The father trekked out to the fields to find out why the elder brother hadn't joined the party, to invite him to join in the celebration.

It's interesting to note the response of the elder brother to the father's invitation.

- He had a sense of entitlement. "You never gave a party for me," he thought. Basically, it's the old response that says, "I'm not getting what I think I deserve," and it was kindled by the fact that the younger son was getting a party thrown in his honour.
- He had a hard work ethic. As I have noted, there's nothing wrong with duty, responsibility, and hard work. The problem is the attitude in which those were done.
- This all led to his contempt for his younger brother. These elements blocked him from accepting the invitation and going inside to welcome home the prodigal and enjoy the party.

Let us return to the image of the party. The crucial and central aspect of this rather powerful story is the extravagant, abundant, and joy-filled love of the father—for both of his sons. There was room in his house for both brothers.

Theologian Helmut Thielicke points this out:

There you have the infinite goodness of the Father. When to men the conversion of the lost appears to be only a cheap capitulation, He sees in it the blessed homecoming of an unhappy soul. And when to men the faithfulness of the elder brother seems nothing more than dull Philistine respectability, He sees in it the dependability of a heart surrendered to him. How broad is the love of the Father! It spans the whole scale of human possibilities. And the wonder of it is that even you and I, with all our peculiarities, have a place in that heart and are safe there![4]

We are all invited to the party in the Father's house! A party is a great image for us of the Christian life, for did not Jesus tell us that he came to offer life in abundance to the full?

That brings me to a great "say what" moment in reconsidering this wonderful story. The elder brother had all his father's love, all the resources and security of the family home, and business available to him every day. He could have had a banquet every night, along with deep sharing with the father of the day's activities, with laughter and song at things that had gone on. But no, something had blocked all that: attitude! What limited the elder brother from fully enjoying life with his father was his own attitude.

That attitude was exposed in his reaction to the return of his brother. Sure, he had worked hard, and probably in doing that he had even expanded the value of the farm, something he would be entitled to receive fully as his inheritance now that the younger son had cashed out his third. But that work had been done with the limitation of his attitude, leaving no place for the satisfaction of joy in a job well done. Only duty remained, and a heavy duty at that. The warning sign of his hardened attitude was the bitterness he expressed both to his father and brother. He showed no grace or joy, just resentment. All those yabbuts!

Jesus indicated that his kingdom was to be one of fullness and great joy. There is a party to be enjoyed. However, too much of the religion of the time, represented by those scribes and Pharisees, exchanged

---

4   Hemut Thielicke, *The Waiting Father* (New York, NY: Harper and Row, 1959), 33.

slavish obedience to heartfelt joy. Instead of rejoicing when a leper was cleansed, they complained that Jesus had healed on the Sabbath. This lack of joy disturbed Jesus so much that he called those religious leaders "whitened sepulchres," appearing holy on the outside but lacking the necessary love on the inside to truly live out the love of God.

This is a forceful reminder to all of us that our Christian lives are to be full of life, love, joy, and celebration. Be very careful when the traditions we build up around the gospel actually block the full flowering of God's love in Jesus. Beware of being that elder brother, who could have enjoyed a loving father every day of his life and rejoiced at the return of his brother but rather sat back, refused any joy, and nursed his own wounded ego. How full is your joy? How joy-filled is your family, your church?

Living Out Our "Say What" Moment

Think about those yabbuts. How many have you entertained throughout your life? How often have you fallen prey to doubts and fears and failed to follow your dreams? Can you face current yabbut limitations in your life? Consider that God has a plan for your life and it is a good one. Not only does he give you the vision, but in faith he will provide the power of the Holy Spirit to carry you to fulfill what he has in mind for you. What dreams or visions do you need to dust off, resisting any yabbuts, and joyfully bring into your life?

Take a few minutes to consider two things: the image of the party of life Jesus is inviting us to enjoy and the limitations you may place on yourself that prevent you from truly experiencing that life. Check your attitudes, watch for any signs of bitterness or resentment of others, and look out for places of fear. We've all put unnecessary, artificial limitations on our lives and faith, but here comes the father out to greet us. There's a party going on and God wants us inside to fully share in all the joy and excitement. How willing are you to head inside?

Think about the party going on in the father's house to celebrate the return of the younger son. There's food, music, laughter, and all that goes with a great, joyful time. I believe that's what Jesus desires for us.

Do our worship times express that joy? A celebration usually involves quite a diversity of people. Do our times of Christian fellowship reflect this? Do we readily join together with all whom God has brought in or do we circulate only with those we know well? Are we uncomfortable with those who dress, act, or look different than us? Are we, like that elder brother, suspicious of the kind of God who so readily forgives? Are we willing to forgive and extend love and welcome?

A Prayer for Living Out Our "Say What" Moment

Father God, in Jesus you promised to bring us life, in abundance, to the full and even overflowing. I realize that I have allowed the fears and doubts of those yabbuts to control too much of my life. I have left dreams unrealized and not always fulfilled what Jesus desires for me. I confess that too often I have been like the elder brother, working away in the fields of life but not with a joyful or generous attitude. So many things in my life can rob me of the joy of serving you.

Remind me that you want life to be full and joy-filled. Restore unto me the excitement of serving you. Help me not to resent any wayward children who are being welcomed back into the family of God. Fill our worship and fellowship with the joy of abundant life. Set us free to truly live and love and serve with all our hearts. May we all truly join in the joy-filled "party" of the kingdom of God. In Jesus's name, amen.

Potential

Chapter Five

LIFE IS FULL OF THE MIRACULOUS, BUT TOO OFTEN WE RUSH PAST OUR daily opportunities to savour the wonder and mystery of God's amazing creation. My wife and I have been blessed with the opportunity to provide ministry through Huron Feathers Presbyterian Centre, a special summer ministry located on a beautiful stretch of white sand beach at Sauble Beach, Ontario. Part of that ministry is an outreach to children and young people who come to this beach for summer vacations.

I like to challenge them to consider the miracles they can observe at such a special place. For example, without the vast array of artificial light so present in our urban areas, they can easily view the starry skies. The galaxy's milky way can be seen on clear summer nights, as well as meteor showers. While lying on the beach, gazing skyward, you can count many of those meteorites flashing across the sky.

Later in summer, we watch monarch butterflies flit along the shore on their way to spend the winter thousands of miles away in Mexico. They fly to a very particular place there and gather in the tens of thousands in trees. How they manage to navigate that journey is truly miraculous. God's creation is just packed with miracles we can observe every day—if we have eyes to see.

One example I like to use with the children comes from an old saying: "Anyone can count the number of seeds in an apple, but only God can count the number of apples in a seed."

Taking an apple, I cut it open and have the children carefully count the seeds inside it. Next, I take one of the seeds and tell them that a vast orchard of apple trees is stored up inside that seed. I add a few details:

- In one seed is a full apple tree, but we must plant it in the ground and wait quite a while for the tree to grow into maturity to the point where it produces apples.
- When the tree from this one seed grows, it will produce apples every year. Let's say it produces thirty apples a year for twenty years. That comes to six hundred apples. And let's say there are eight seeds in every apple. That adds up to 240 seeds per year, times twenty years, resulting in a possible 4,800 apple trees.
- We like to eat apples, so let's say we keep only ten apples per year to plant, eating the rest. That gives us ten apples times eight seeds per apple, times twenty years, which equals 1,600 apple trees over twenty years. That's a lot of apple trees!
- Consider just what those trees could produce. 1,600 trees. with thirty apples per tree every year, would produce forty-eight thousand apples. If each apple had eight seeds, that would add up to a potential 544,000 apple trees. Now that's what I consider a rather mighty miracle of God's creation! And remember: all of this potential is inside *one* apple seed.

Jesus was very aware of the miraculous power of growth. Drawing from examples from creation—seeds and yeast, for example—he applied growth principles to his teachings on the kingdom of God. Thus, a number of these simple parables begin with "The kingdom of God is like..."

Let us explore both the examples drawn from everyday experience and the way we can apply these truths to our understanding of the kingdom of God.

THE POTENTIAL OF THE HARVEST
READ MARK 4:26-29

Those listening to Jesus would have been very familiar with planting and harvesting. Their lives depended on these seasons. They knew well that a seed has the potential of a rich harvest, and once planted the process of growth begins. We, too, depend on that process even though we're often quite removed from it as we consume the produce of the land without thinking about or thanking God for his provision.

The important thing to recognize here is that this miraculous potential is totally dependent on the creative power of God. The farmer in the parable plants the seeds, then waits until the ripened grain is ready for harvest. The farmer didn't create the potential in the seed; it was God.

Applying this first growth principle to the kingdom of God also reinforces some basic truths. First, there is tremendous potential in those teachings of Jesus to bring about God's kingdom on this earth. Simple little lessons like these develop that truth: from small beginnings can come the eventual flowering of the fullness of the kingdom. It is important for us to grasp this potential and not negate the seemingly small and powerless actions we might take for Jesus.

God has placed the potential for growth in the seed, but to grow the seed it must be planted. I would like to draw out the importance of the partnership between the sower and the seed. In kingdom principles, this reinforces the necessity of taking the first step in sowing the love and peace of Jesus. Everything has a beginning, and we can be that beginning. Each effort will have a future result.

We often crave an immediate result. However, in the economy of the kingdom, longer-term growth is essential. We may not even be present or aware of the future harvest. Another worker in the kingdom may reap the harvest we have sown. Nevertheless, it is important for us to realize that there won't be a harvest without our acts of sowing. Jesus continually taught and encouraged the twelve he chose to follow him. They didn't always see dramatic or immediate results, yet what Jesus sowed in those individuals continues to bear the fruit of growing the kingdom of God.

We are part of the growth Jesus began with the disciples. We can all trace our heritage in the faith back to those original disciples of Jesus. Consider the impact of the kingdom growth that has taken place. Be amazed at the growth that's happening now around the globe, particularly in Africa and Asia. The potential of so many seeds of faith being brought to harvest, and the potential of seeds of faith continually being sown, is truly miraculous. Praise God!

THE MUSTARD SEED
READ MATTHEW 13:31-34, MARK 4:30-33, LUKE 13:18-19

Jesus continues to develop his teaching on the growth potential of the kingdom of God in his parable of the mustard seed. In it, He contrasts the small size of the seed and its potential to grow into a tree large enough for birds to perch, and even build nests, in its branches. From small beginnings come amazing results. It would appear that Jesus was countering the messianic expectations of his day, that a powerful messiah would appear who would re-establish Israel as a powerful earthly kingdom to the way it had been in the time of King David. For the people of Jesus's time, this would involve the overthrow of the Roman occupiers and give control of the land back to Israel.

Jesus came proclaiming that the kingdom of God had already come upon the earth. But for many, a simple rabbi from Galilee and a small group of disciples certainly didn't appear to fulfill the messianic hope. It appeared to be too small and insignificant a beginning. It certainly appeared that Rome was firmly in control. You get the sense, reading the gospels, that the disciples were wondering just when the sudden and powerful reversal of history would strike.

The reality is that Jesus didn't come to invoke a top-down kingdom under the control of a powerful new king. Instead, he began building a bottom-up kingdom, a kingdom of the heart by those who responded to his invitation, person by person. Seeds of the kingdom were being planted from which God would bring growth and the kingdom would expand. Eventually, like a full-grown mustard plant, the kingdom would emerge.

In his writings, Helmut Thieliicke draws out the bottom-up ministry of Jesus:

> [Jesus] has time to stop and talk to the individual. He associates with publicans, lonely widows, and despised prostitutes; he moves among the outcasts of society, wrestling for the soul of individuals. He appears not to be bothered at all by the fact that these are not strategically important people, that they have no prominence, that they are not key figures, but only the unfortunate, lost children of the Father in heaven. He seems to ignore with a sovereign indifference the great so-called "world-historical perspectives" of his mission when it comes to one insignificant, blind and smelly beggar, this Mr. Nobody, who is nevertheless so dear to the heart of God and must be saved.[5]

A farmer plants seeds in faith that the potential locked inside that seed will be released and bring forth a harvest. God holds the creative power, but it's the farmer who exercises faith by planting the seed. The person who plants a mustard seed has hope in the vision of the full-grown mustard plant and the birds flocking to its shelter. Jesus spoke of this mustard-seed faith; we may see no immediate results, yet seeds are planted in faith.

When we feel that our own small mustard seeds of faith, daily actions of love and care, and routines of serving seem insignificant, we are encouraged to keep on planting in the faith that God honours the potential sown by each act of service. God holds the creative power in those acts to build his kingdom. It is to us, his followers, that he gives daily opportunities to plant those seeds of faith.

THE YEAST METAPHOR
READ MATTHEW 13:33, LUKE 13:20

Jesus turns to another common element, yeast, to point out another kingdom principle. Yeast, or leaven, is an essential element for baking.

---

5 Thielicke, *The Waiting Father*, 88–89.

At the time of Jesus, it was the custom when baking bread for a small portion of the risen dough to be kept for the next batch. When it was put into a new batch of dough, the fermentation would slowly spread throughout the mass. The yeast literally changed the ingredients, creating the means for bread to rise properly and taste good.

☞ The point Jesus is getting at here is the power of yeast to infiltrate the entire mass of dough, producing growth that's not initially visible. The imperceptible power of the rising dough is another act of faith, this time by the baker. The baker exercises faith in the power of yeast to produce the necessary rising for a fine loaf of bread.

We, too, in living out our faith in the potential of God to transform the world, act as that leaven. Jesus leavens us with his word and truth, and then we, in applying that word and truth, leaven the world around us. Once again, we count on the potential God has provided. God will bring about the growth of his kingdom, just like yeast. Remember, too, that even if it doesn't appear visible at first, the leaven of the kingdom is continually working. Trust God: there will be results!

THE SOWING OF THE SEEDS
READ LUKE 8:4-15

Jesus told another parable about sowing seeds. In this parable, the emphasis lies upon the nature of the soils into which the seeds are sown. The one sowing the seed scattered it over a large expanse, including a variety of soil conditions. Some fell on the pathway where it was stepped on and the birds ate it up. No growth occurred there. Other seed fell on rocky ground; these plants sprouted, but there was insufficient nourishment and they withered. Some seed fell among thorn bushes which choked the growth of the seed. Finally, some seed did end up in fertile soil and produced a great yield.

In this parable, Jesus takes time to provide a detailed explanation. It can also be taken as an allegory, with each item in the story relating to a specific point of truth. The variety of soils represents the conditions of the hearts of those who hear the teachings of Jesus. The birds represent the devil, who steals the Word of God from those who have heard it. The rocky soil represents those who initially accept the Word but don't let it sink deep into them; they fall away when they are first tested. Thorn bushes represent the cares and concerns of the world which choke out the seed of the kingdom. Finally, there is the fertile soil (representing those who open their hearts and lives to Jesus) into which the seed is sown, grows, and provides a rich harvest.

We can easily identify with all of these conditions. Perhaps at times we have been like rocky soil or allowed the thorn bushes of worry to choke out the love of Jesus in our lives. Despite the various conditions of these soils, the sower scatters the seed into all. The sower has faith in his seed, faith that despite the amount of seed lost to bad conditions there will be enough sown into fertile ground to provide a harvest. Our act of faith in the seed of Jesus's love and teaching is to be faithful in sowing. We are called to sow into all soils, having faith in the power of the seed to grow.

I would even go further, to say that at times seed will sprout and flourish even in the most adverse conditions. We've all seen a flower sprouting through a crack in the pavement. Often the shoots of a new tree will pop up where the old tree has been cut or fallen down. Therefore, we must continue to sow as far and wide as we can, allowing God to bring about growth.

Living Out Our "Say What" Moment

Take some time today to rediscover your sense of wonder. Perhaps get up early enough to enjoy the sunrise and then pause at the end of the day to take in the setting sun. Open your eyes wide to a passing butterfly and marvel at the intricate beauty of its wings. As night grows darker, step outside to look up (if there is not too much artificial light) and consider the stars overhead, which is God's masterpiece extending far with its billions of galaxies. Perhaps you can make out the milky way, or perhaps some of the planets like Venus, the "evening star." You might be fortunate enough to be surprised by a shooting star or dazzled by the dancing colours of the northern lights. God truly is an amazing Creator!

With your senses open to behold the wonder of God's creation, now look for signs of growth. If it's spring, watch for the first shoots and wildflowers. In summer, stop to contemplate the growing crops, the sunflowers shooting their flowers high into the sky. In fall, as you enjoy the changing colours of the leaves, realize that God protects those trees by having the life-giving chlorophyll retreat to the roots for the winter. In winter, pause to remember that seeds are lying in wait under the snow, that animals are hibernating and that next year's butterflies are safely protected in cocoons awaiting the spring warmth. Be amazed at what God provides!

God has created you. Like the seed that has immense potential inside, God has placed unique gifts and abilities in you. There is no other you. Glorify God for that! Is that potential still locked up inside you? Are you growing in your faith? Is there more of God's creation inside of you to be discovered and allowed to grow? What steps might you take to unlock more of your God-given potential? Have you prepared the "soil" of your life to allow those seeds to grow? Or are there the thorn bushes of cares, worries, and fears choking your growth? Has life hardened you like the rocky soil, so any growth is short-lived? Have birds of hurt and abuse carried away your true self and left disappointment and despair behind? How can you better prepare the soil of your life to receive God's truth and will for your life?

Look for signs of the growth of the kingdom of God. Are seeds of faith sprouting? Is some of the growth ready for harvest? Is the church you attend alive and growing in God's Word? God's love and power should be working like leaven to fill the fellowship with grace, peace, and love. What are the signs that the leaven is working? What seeds of faith in Jesus are being sown in the community around you? Remember that the sower casts seed far and wide. God will grow those seeds. The leaven of God's love that you extend into your community will work and grow.

A Prayer for Living Out Our "Say What" Moment

Lord God, I live in a universe of wonder and majesty. Your creative power is alive all around me. I admit that far too often I hurry through life, missing the amazing miracles you have placed before me every day. Open my eyes to behold the beauty of even the smallest of flowers. May I listen for the song of birds and the laughter of children. May I savour the gifts of sight and sound and touch you provide for me constantly.

Lord, I am a miracle. There is only one unique me. May I truly appreciate what you have created in me, the potential of gifts and abilities and talents with which you have gifted me. Unlock all of that, Lord, if I have for too long lived without the seeds of your life in me sprouting, growing, and producing fruit. Move aside the brambles of care and concern, and soften the hard places within me that block your growth. Enable me to withstand any attack by the devil that would steal your word of truth in my life. Breathe your Spirit of life into me so that I will always be growing, loving, and serving you. Open my eyes to discover those around me who need my encouragement and care.

Together with sisters and brothers in the faith, challenge us to sow seeds and mix the leaven of Jesus's love and grace into our communities and world. We trust you, Lord, to bring about the harvest. In Jesus's name, amen.

Priorities

Chapter Six

I HAVE HEARD AND USED A MODERN PARABLE ON A NUMBER OF OCCASIONS. It's called "The Lifesaving Station," and here's one version of that story.

There was a dangerous stretch of seacoast where shipwrecks were all too common. A small, rustic lifesaving station had been built there, but it only had one lifeboat. A dedicated crew kept watch, and when necessary they set out in the lifeboat to rescue those who were shipwrecked. They saved many lives. In fact, news of this little station grew and many new people came to lend a hand. With extra help, they acquired new lifeboats and the rescuers received better training.

As time went on, some of the station's crewmembers were unhappy to still be using the original rustic shack and felt that something more substantial would be better. A more comfortable station would provide better relief for those who had been pulled from the waters. So they built a new station, larger, more comfortable, and better equipped. The crew furnished it well and it became a kind of club, a gathering place for many.

Due to this new, more comfortable station, fewer members of the crew were interested in going out on rescue missions.

Around this time, a large ship wrecked off the coast and the crew carried in many cold, wet, and half-drowned people. However, many crewmembers became upset at the wet, soggy mess the survivors left behind. So they built a shower house outside so that victims could be cleaned up before entering the station.

This led to a division in the membership. It turned out that a majority wanted to cease active lifesaving activities, as it had become a hindrance to their social lives. Some members pointed out that the original purpose of the station was to rescue drowning victims of shipwrecks, but they were voted down.

Those few crewmembers who were loyal to the original mission started a new, struggling lifesaving station down the coast. The lights of their little station blazed brightly as they remained faithful to rescuing people struggling in the waves and weather.

Sadly, far too many people drowned in shipwrecks on that coast, with not enough crewmembers to rescue them.

There's quite an important lesson to be learned here. We've all experienced that human tendency for our priorities in life to get jumbled, allowing for lesser items to overtake what should have been most important. We too often choose to major in the minors of life. It takes effort and discipline to maintain our priorities. Too often, our desire for comfort tends to override the more demanding but rewarding priorities of our faith.

The parable of the lifesaving station illustrates how both we as individuals and our churches can be tempted to shift our priorities away from our original zeal to serve Jesus. Consider your life. What are your priorities? Have they changed or shifted over the years? Are you truly able, as Matthew 6:33 says, to seek first the kingdom of God?

THE TREASURE IN THE FIELD
READ MATTHEW 13:44

In Jesus's time, it wasn't unusual for someone wishing to hide some wealth to simply bury it. Then, if something happened to him, that treasure might remain hidden in the ground for some time. In this brief story, Jesus presents an individual who stumbled upon such a treasure buried in a field. Note that this man didn't own that field.

The man liquidated all his assets to buy the field and claim the treasure. Jewish law at the time didn't state that anything found belonged to the finder. We shouldn't get too exercised about whether the treasure rightfully should have been declared to the original owner of the field. The point of the story, its "say what" moment, is the willingness of the man who discovered the treasure to do everything in his power to acquire the field and claim the treasure.

This parable relates to Jesus's teaching about placing first our efforts to seek after the kingdom of God. Those who prioritize discovering and living out the life and teachings of Jesus are willing to make sacrifices in order to receive the great joy that comes with living in the kingdom. The man in the parable recognized the potential value of the treasure and went all-out to claim it.

Placing our priority in life on the most valuable thing—the kingdom that Jesus offers to us—enables us to expend the effort needed to gain that kingdom. We must seek, knock, and ask to find what might otherwise remain dormant, like an underground treasure.

Note also that this seeking will be rewarded. Placing our priority on making a decision to follow Jesus will bring a reward. Jesus tells us that if we seek first the kingdom of God and his righteousness, all other things necessary for our lives will be given to us. The man who found the treasure experienced great joy in acquiring the great treasure. So will we, if our priorities are right.

The treasure for the man in the parable really was a gift. He didn't work for it, but rather he discovered it. The importance lies in his effort to claim the gift.

Jesus offers us life in abundance, to the full, a full life now and eternally. What a wonderful gift! But like any gift, we must receive it and accept it, which may demand some sacrifice from us as we shift our priorities. As we shall see in another parable, our material standards may need to change, our investments reorganized, our use of time and abilities moved to new areas of service. Rewards will come with this effort.

THE PEARL OF GREAT PRICE
READ MATTHEW 13:45-46

In this second short story, a pearl merchant discovers a pearl that to his eyes is the most precious and valuable he has ever laid eyes on. In ancient times, as now, pearls were greatly desired and thus became a standard of value and wealth. However, this pearl was so precious that it demanded a high price tag. Its value was obvious to all. That didn't deter the merchant, but he had to sell all he had to purchase it. He had a single purpose, a number one priority which guided his action.

What is the great pearl in our lives? Jesus told this parable to indicate that the kingdom of God is this great and most valuable thing. Too often we settle for "lesser pearls," such as pleasures, popularity, and momentary satisfaction.

As with the treasure in the field, the point of the parable lies in the ability of the pearl merchant to go after what was the most valuable thing in his life. Are we as willing to go all-out in our seeking of the kingdom of God? Or are we content with those lesser pearls of life?

Again, our priorities are challenged. And again, we can experience great joy when the pearl is acquired. Great joy will be ours if we place our priorities on seeking to experience God's loving will for our lives and living out the abundant life that Jesus has promised us!

THE LILIES OF THE FIELD AND BIRDS OF THE AIR
READ MATTHEW 6:24–34

Let us return for a moment to the underlying teaching of Jesus regarding setting our priority in life on seeking the kingdom of God. In this passage from the Sermon on the Mount, Jesus addresses what lies at the root of our often mixed-up priorities: anxiety and worry.

Like us today, people in Jesus's day were constantly anxious about food, clothing, and possessions, causing them to strive after those things. Jesus points to the lilies of the field and the birds of the air, for whom God provides. Will he not also provide for us?

Jesus admonishes us to trust in God, who cares for his children like any loving father. By placing our faith in his ability to provide for us, we can maintain kingdom priorities, such as maintaining loving relationships in our families, churches, and communities and seeking to support those around us who have great need.

The key, of course, is having faith in the loving, caring God revealed through Jesus. Jesus certainly maintained the priorities of the kingdom, making himself constantly available to heal, encourage, and restore all those whom he met along the pathways of Galilee. We should make loving relationships our priority: loving God, loving our neighbours, and loving ourselves.

THE RICH FOOL
READ LUKE 12:13-21

Jesus addressed the priorities of life in his parable of the rich fool. He told this story of a successful farmer as a response to a question posed to him regarding the division of an inheritance: *"Teacher, tell my brother to divide with me the property our father left us."* Jesus refused to step into this family dispute and take sides. Rather, he perceived the heart of the man who posed the question, finding there covetousness and greed. Warning against such emotions, Jesus told the following story.

A rich man had been blessed with fertile land which produced bumper crops. This created a problem, for he didn't have sufficient storehouses for all the grain. So he decided to build bigger ones. In doing this, he congratulated himself for the future when he would reap the benefit from all this wealth. His goal was to take life easy, then eat, drink, and enjoy himself.

Now, that might seem to be a worthwhile perspective, certainly in current terms of investment.

Some commentators point out that this man had reaped great benefit from his fertile fields. He probably had good business sense. But rather than sharing his great harvest, he only desired to store it up. He would continue to benefit from being the one to control the amount of grain available on the local market and the price of that produce. Those paying his prices wouldn't necessarily feel as satisfied or enjoy the same level of ease and comfort.

This appears to be a continual situation for humanity.

As Jesus develops this story, the issue appears to be one of selfishness and greed, for the farmer thinks only of himself. He congratulates himself for his foresight in setting himself up for an easy retirement. There is no sense whatsoever of gratitude to God for the blessings of a rich harvest. The warning, of course, comes in the man's misplaced priorities on wealth and material possessions.

The rich man died suddenly, and all that he had worked so hard to achieve during his life became useless to him. Perhaps his living relatives would fight to see who got the most of all that stored-up wealth.

Jesus rightfully reminds us that if building up material possessions and wealth are the only priorities in our lives, they can and will disappear in an instant. We can't take it with us upon death.

RICHES IN HEAVEN
READ MATTHEW 6:19-21

Let us return to the dynamic teaching of Jesus in his Sermon on the Mount. This passage gives light to the parable of the rich fool. Jesus reminds us about ultimate priorities, advising us to lay up our treasure not on earth, where it can decay or be stolen, but to instead lay up treasure in heaven. I'm sure Jesus is referring to setting our priorities to loving relationships over the anxious striving for material wealth or status. The rich fool forgot that. Despite worldly success, his eternal legacy of care and love would be paltry.

Jesus provides a great way to check out where our priorities stand: *"For your heart will always be where your riches are"* (Matthew 6:21). Worldly wealth may appear wonderful, but in the long run, as Jesus points out, *"Do not store up riches for yourselves here on earth, where moths and rust destroy, and robbers break in and steal"* (Matthew 6:19). Therefore, are we wise or foolish?

One way to consider just how much treasure we're laying up in our heavenly account is to think about the legacy we will one day leave behind. What might be said about you at your funeral? Will there be a great testimony to how you've changed lives, built your community, served your church, and nurtured your family? For the rich fool in the parable, it would appear that the only testimony to him was that he was rich, which is not much of a legacy. If he had lived, he would have used all that he had accumulated to enable a continuing selfish lifestyle of ease and comfort. He could have done so much more with what God had given him.

What about you?

Living Out Our "Say What" Moment

Consider the investments of your life. At this point in your life, where is your time, talent, and treasury being invested?

Time. Is your time being well used for what matters most in your life? Review your past week. What set the priorities for your time? Did you have enough time for nurturing the relationships in your life? How much time did you set aside for your spiritual growth—worship, prayer, bible study, etc.? Were you able to invest time to care for others, such as in your community and church? Did you invest time in building yourself up by exercising, walking, and enjoying God's creation? Did old habits divert you into wasting time? Did you miss opportunities to invest time in renewing priorities you may have let slip? For example, did you write that note you've been intending to write, make that phone call to inquire about the health of an old friend, express thanks to someone who has invested in your life, or seek forgiveness of someone whom you have caused hurt? There are so many important ways to invest our time, so you need to set priorities. Are you seeking first the kingdom of God?

Talent. How well are your gifts and talents being used? A constant theme in this book is God's love, his creative power in you for building his kingdom, and the gifts, talents, and resources he has placed in you to enable you to grow your part of that kingdom. How aware are you of these truths? How can you better apply these truths to your situation?

Remember the lifesaving station parable. Are the talents of those in your church being directed at growing God's kingdom and proclaiming the gospel of Jesus in word and action, or is too much time being invested in busyness or in maintaining the appearance of the church and not the heart and soul of serving Jesus? In what ways can all of us called by Jesus into his kingdom seek first that kingdom?

Treasury. How are you prioritizing your own material wealth? I know there are so many demands on our money these days, but it's always important to review and reset budgets where possible. Out of gratitude to God's loving providence for your life, have you made it a priority to contribute to the ongoing work of the ministry and mission of Jesus, hopefully tithing? Remember that our joyful giving unto God will bring the growth of his kingdom and the fruit of blessing.

Do you give in to impulse buying? Are you accumulating too much debt? Does your investment of your material goods match your investment in loving relationships? How do your finances enable you to care for others? How well are your material resources seeking first the kingdom of God? What will be your legacy?

A Prayer for Living Out Our "Say What" Moment

Lord God, I take a few minutes to review all that you have given me. I begin with the realization that everything I have—all my time, talents, and material goods—has come from you. Lord, too often I take all this for granted. Sometimes I glorify in myself, that it is me who has done so much and acquired so much.

Forgive me, Lord, and correct my perspective. Enable me to set my priorities on furthering your kingdom. Help me to put relationships before striving to do more or get more. Remind me of what will be of ultimate value that I may offer of myself what truly will make a difference for my family, friends, church, community, and world. Quiet my anxieties about life by reminding me that as I seek what's most important, building your kingdom of love and grace, you, our loving Father, will provide all that I truly need in life. May I live in a more trusting relationship with you, loving God. In Jesus's name, amen.

Persistence

Chapter Seven

I ONCE HEARD A TRUE STORY THAT SERVES AS AN ILLUSTRATION OF persistence. A woman named Martha Berry, who lived in the early part of the twentieth century in the American state of Georgia, had a deep underlying passion to teach and train poor children in the northern part of that state who had no access to education. However, Martha possessed no books, no building, and no money, just her dream and passion. So she began to work out how to fulfill her dream. She started by teaching Sunday school to children in an abandoned church. That led to her opening a boarding school for boys. She began with five boys but saw both the need and the potential for more.

When the school was struggling for funds, Martha spent time and energy approaching potential supporters of her cause. Here's where the story gets interesting. It is told that she travelled to Detroit to seek the support of Henry Ford. She boldly asked him for one million dollars, which Ford, the great automobile entrepreneur, could easily afford. However, Ford, weary of the rather constant requests for financial support, reached into his pocket and said, "Look, here is one dime. That's all the money I have in my pocket, but you can have it."

Say what? Most of us, including me, would have been insulted and discouraged. We might have said, "Well, God, it would appear that my dream just isn't going to work out. Perhaps I should return home and live a quiet life."

Instead of giving up, Martha Berry demonstrated the unique staying power of persistence. She used that dime from Henry Ford to plant a small crop of peanuts and used the first harvest from that crop to plant even more peanuts. Remember the illustration of the apple seed in a previous chapter?

Martha faithfully sent Ford a detailed accounting of each year's harvest, and eventually it paid off. Ford was so impressed by Martha Berry's faithful persistence that he visited her school and donated the one million dollars and more! Ford began providing buildings for the growing campus.

Martha died in 1942, but due to her faithful persistence in following her dream Berry College is now a private four-year college with 1,700 students enrolled. Recently, the Ford Foundation gave the school a $94 million dollar grant—the culmination of one small dime turning into the fulfillment of a God-given dream and the persistence to carry it through!

Let us now take a look at some rather unusual stories told by Jesus to encourage his followers to exercise persistence in their faith walk and prayer lives.

THE PERSISTENT WIDOW
READ LUKE 18:1-8

To begin with, we need to remember that a parable makes a basic point. Not every detail in the story can be deciphered. The judge in this story is essential to the narrative, creating a dramatic "say what" response, but make sure you don't extend your analysis to figure that the judge represents God in any respect. This judge neither feared God nor cared about people.

Also remember that most of Jesus's parables were initially told in a specific setting and situation. Luke records that this story, of an unrighteous judge and a persistent widow, was told in response to the potential discouragement of the followers of Jesus that the kingdom wasn't being fully realized as they hoped it might. Certainly by the time Luke wrote his gospel, the early church was undergoing significant persecution. This parable, finds theologian Fred Craddock, presumes an audience that has been taught to pray, "Thy kingdom come" but has been experiencing persecution and hardship and as a result begins to "lose heart." By Luke's day, several generations had passed since Jesus had taught his disciples to pray, and enthusiasm and faithfulness can be eroded by time alone, as well as by suffering and abuse.[6]

The story, which Jesus tells to encourage his followers and us today, is really intriguing. Honesty and integrity were highly valued traits in judges in Jewish society. This judge, who had no regard for God or anyone else, was a real villain. A widow in that society faced an uncertain life. Without a male relative to take her in, she would be vulnerable and defenceless. She had no say and no way to stand up for herself. Perhaps her opponent in this story was a male relative who was expected to assist her but had refused. Even the judge refused to act on her behalf.

She could have just given up, but this widow was tough. She refused to give in. This parable sets up a surprise ending: the widow literally wore down the judge until he finally relented, fearing that she would just keep coming back again and again. Her persistence paid off.

Another storytelling technique employed by Jesus in this parable arises from a reasoning from lesser to greater. If a corrupt judge will grant justice to a poor widow (lesser), how much more would God grant our requests (greater)? Remember Jesus's counsel to us to be persistent in asking, seeking, and knocking. Jesus isn't advocating for us to constantly beg God for answers. He's advocating for us not to give up when our requests don't seem to be immediately granted. We must retain faith in God's eventual vindication, just as the widow didn't give up until she was satisfied.

The reality is that at times it may appear that our asking, seeking, and knocking is futile. That should be a call for even more persistence. We can trust in a loving God whose desire is to bless us. Unfortunately, other people's actions, situations, and circumstances may block that

---

6   Fred Craddock, *Interpretation: A Bible Commentary for Teaching and Preaching— Luke* (Louisville, KY: John Knox Press, 1990), 209.

blessing. Faithful persistence in the present creates the opportunity for a future answer. This may require great effort and patience on our part.

Craddock quotes an elderly black preacher who gave a one-sentence interpretation of this parable: "Unless you have stood for years knocking at a locked door, your knuckles bleeding, you do not really know what prayer is."[7]

We would all like to have our prayers dramatically and instantly answered. Sometimes they are and we rejoice. Other times, we seem to hear nothing but silence. At that point, do we abandon our prayers? Certainly that can be the temptation: "Well, I tried praying about that, but I got nowhere!" Jesus advocates persistence, not resignation, in those situations.

At times I have realized that the very situation I was praying for God to intervene in had already been laid in my hands to deal with. I had just figured that God could sort it out quicker than I could, so I resisted doing what I knew was necessary. Other times, persisting in prayer has allowed me to gain a different perspective on the situation, meaning that I had to give God lots of opportunities to speak to me! I needed to listen as much as to lay all my needs and concerns before him. Staying persistent in prayer anchors me to God's Word, reinforcing my relationship with God and opening me to truly embrace his loving will for my life. No matter what my present situation, I can rely on God's promise that he knows the plans he has for us and holds a future and a hope for each of us (Jeremiah 29:11).

I have come to truly value those whom we call prayer warriors, those will take an individual's cause and pray, sometimes for years. Prayer is vitally needed for many situations in our world, and it seems prayer will be needed forever. Prayer warriors lift up the persecuted church, the refugees, the starving and neglected children, the wars, the persecutions and abuse... the list seems endless. But we are all called to prayer, even if it might seem wearying to us. We must pray that prayer of Jesus, "Thy kingdom come," for a lifetime. Let us be persistent in doing just that!

---

7   Ibid., 210.

A FRIEND AT MIDNIGHT
READ LUKE 11:5-8

Jesus told a second parable about demonstrating persistent faith in prayer. The disciples had requested to be coached in prayer, *"just as John taught his disciples"* (Luke 11:11). Jesus responded by teaching them the prayer we know as the Lord's Prayer. He then continued with the story of a friend at midnight. Again, it's an intriguing story with an essential central point: God is not to be compared to a sleepy friend who gives in to a persistent neighbour.

Hospitality was expected in the Middle East, so when a guest arrived late and there wasn't food, the would-be host had to go out and secure some. Neighbours were also expected to assist in this hospitality if they had anything to share. Instead, the neighbour in this story shuttered his house; the family was asleep and it would appear that the neighbour intended it to stay that way. However, the would-be host simply banged and banged on the door until the weary neighbour had to give in.

This is yet another of those "lesser to greater" parables. If the stingy neighbour can be convinced to finally provide some bread, how much more can our heavenly Father, who in love desires the best for us, be counted on to provide our needs?

This goes back to the teaching of Jesus in the Sermon on the Mount regarding asking, seeking, and knocking. Jesus elaborates with the example of a human parent, contrasting this with how much more a loving God desires to provide for us:

> *Would any of you who are fathers give your son a stone when he asks for bread? Or would you give him a snake when he asks for a fish? As bad as you are, you know how to give good things to your children. How much more, then, will your Father in heaven give good things to those who ask him!*
> —Matthew 7:9–11

I would like to offer one final note regarding the parables of the persistent widow and the friend at midnight. In both cases, the disciples are waiting for the full culmination of the kingdom Jesus came to usher in. For them, and for those reading Luke's gospel today, it would seem that this culmination has been delayed. We may be weary of waiting, but do we give up? We don't know when it will come, but come it will, and we are called to keep our persistent faithfulness until that day when Jesus returns.

Luke created his gospel to encourage us in going through trials and persecutions. We are to be faithful and persistent in our walk of faith. No matter the circumstance we find ourselves in, we are to persist in prayer. Vindication will come and all wrongs will be put right. In the meantime, we are to trust in God's constant faithfulness in giving us strength and hope: *"But will the Son of Man find faith on earth when he comes?"* (Luke 18:8)

Living Out Our "Say What" Moment

How is your prayer life at this point in time? For whom are you being persistent in prayer? What needs are you currently lifting up? Can you take the necessary time to listen for God rather than doing all the communicating from your side only? Can you persist in prayer to enable those prayers to change in the process? Remember to anchor your prayers in scripture and to go over the promises of God contained there, for his Word will not return empty; it will accomplish what God desires (Isaiah 55:11). Open yourself to the Holy Spirit, who will direct and guide you, providing the wisdom you need for your life.

Think back: when in the past have you given up too easily with prayer? How have you dealt with prayers that appeared not to be heard or answered? Were you open to how God might direct you to deal with the situation for which you were praying? Are there people or situations right now that you need to start persistently praying for again?

There is a widely circulated reading that has been attributed to Mother Teresa. It directs us to the virtues of persistence. The version I have used goes like this:

People are often unreasonable, irrational, and self-centered. Forgive them anyway.

If you are kind, people may accuse you of selfish, ulterior motives. Be kind anyway.

If you are successful, you will win some unfaithful friends and some genuine enemies. Succeed anyway.

If you are honest and sincere people may deceive you. Be honest and sincere anyway.

What you spend years creating, others could destroy overnight. Create anyway.

If you find serenity and happiness, some may be jealous. Be happy anyway.

The good you do today, will often be forgotten. Do good anyway.

Give the best you have, and it will never be enough. Give your best anyway.

In the final analysis, it is between you and God. It was never between you and them anyway.[8]

Too often in our churches we fail to be persistent in prayer. What situations or individuals in your fellowship are crying out for active prayer? Do you pray once and just let those people or situations go, as other needs arise? How can a congregation truly carry through in prayer? How equipped are the members of your church to stop and pray with anyone in need, or is that left up to the clergy? How might the entire body of Christ in a congregation develop strength and persistence in prayer for one another? Does the community around your church realize that they can come, express their needs, and receive prayer? If not, how might that be developed where you are?

8　Mother Teresa, "Do It Anyway," *Prayer Foundation*. Date of access: March 20, 2018 (http://prayerfoundation.org/mother_teresa_do_it_anyway.htm).

A Prayer for Living Out Our "Say What" Moment

Lord God, you provide such a wonderful way of being in relationship with you, through your Word and prayer. Thank you, Lord, for hearing this prayer today. I do crave your presence in my life. Remind me that you desire to share in all my celebrations, sufferings, joys, and sorrows. You care for me, Lord. I admit that I have often neglected this wonderful opportunity to spend time in fellowship with you. Life gets hectic and I fail to stop and take time for you.

I remember times when I haven't felt your answer to my cries. I realize that I have allowed myself to become too easily discouraged. I haven't persisted in prayer and in keeping in touch with you. Enable me to take time with you, to open my heart but also to pause so that I may listen to what you want to say to me. Give me patience to wait for an answer. Help me to receive that answer in whatever way it may come. Strengthen my faith to hold fast to you through my doubts and struggles, to give you the opportunity to come to my side. Enable me to see myself as you see me, to view my circumstances in light of your love, to trust in your abiding care for me. Lord, I put my trust in you. In Jesus's name, amen.

Risk

Chapter Eight

YOU'VE PROBABLY HEARD THE TERM "COMFORT ZONE." WE ALL HAVE ONE. Everything that's familiar and safe acts like a cushion around us and we hold it close. Sometimes too close, as we realize when something new and unfamiliar presents itself. Are we willing to attempt a new venture? Do we take a daring step in a direction we've never tried before? You can know when you approach the edge of your comfort zone: you experience fear and anxiety.

At times our comfort zones keep us safe and prevent us from doing something dangerous. But too often those same comfort zones block us from fulfilling a dream, exploring a new possibility, reaching out to people who are different or challenging to us, and living out the potential God has for our lives. How often has fear and anxiety blocked your journey? Are you truly willing to take a risk to enable God to do a new work in your life?

Over the years, I've had the privilege of meeting some very courageous people willing to take risks for their faith. People whose faith led them far afield. People for whom risk was but a daily experience. People who had left their comfort zones far behind. People whose lives have challenged me to dare to dream God's dream for my life and take the necessary risks to bring those dreams into living reality.

One such adventurer in faith was Lillian Dickson. She was of such small physical stature that I needed to find a box for her to stand on when she arrived at my church to speak. However, once she began telling her stories of great faith, the essence of this woman of faith stood tall. She well deserved the nickname she had been given: Typhoon Lil.

Lillian was born in Prior Lake, Minnesota in 1901. In 1927, after attending the University of Minnesota and a Bible institute, she married Jim Dickson, who was then a student at Princeton Theological Seminary. Jim was commissioned by the Board of Foreign Missions of the Presbyterian Church in Canada as a missionary to Taiwan (then known as Formosa). There he established the Taipei Theological Seminary,

After a number of years of serving as a traditional missionary's wife, Lillian felt challenged by God to address the needs of the land, particularly amongst the aboriginal mountain people. Leprosy, tuberculosis, and other diseases were rampant. The mountain people, such as the Tyal tribe, who had been head-hunters up until just a few years before, were being pushed further and further into the mountains due to the incoming Chinese.

Lillian desired to take education, medical care, and the gospel of Jesus to these people. However, at that time the Presbyterian Church didn't commission wives for missionary service. No problem for Lillian: she began her own mission, which grew in the same manner as the title she gave it—the Mustard Seed Mission.

Lillian came to truly love the people of those mountains, even though the mountains could also be dangerous. Her forays to minister to the people often required considerable risk. Her faith carried her through. She wrote about one particular trip when a sudden typhoon hit. The small group she was with had reached the village of Giok-li, but they realized the village had become totally surrounded by floodwaters. Only an old dam held back a lake further up the mountain, and it was rising with the flood. The dam, however, hadn't been repaired for twenty years, and it posed an immediate threat of breaching.

After being trapped for some time, Lillian and her small group attempted to make their way up the mountain. Many of them felt that it was dangerous, and at best they would end up stranded there for months. Most of the bridges had been washed away or made precarious due to the underpinnings being severely damaged by the floodwaters. Lillian recounts:

> At one place a huge, wide, iron bridge had been washed from its moorings downstream where it was upended on one side, swaying in the rushing current. We had to climb up thirty feet in the air and edge cautiously along its upper edge, barefoot, as they thought we might slip if we wore shoes. On the opposite bank we could see the aborigines watching. "They are either praying for us or laying wagers as to whether or not we will get across alive," I whispered.[9]

Lillian made it that time and many, many more times after that, establishing churches and clinics in countless mountain villages. I'm not sure how I would have fared in similar situations, but when I sense that God is calling me to venture in faith and take risks for Jesus, and I'm tempted to retreat into my comfort zone, I remember the faith of Lillian Dickson, through whom God created a mighty witness to the love of Jesus from her "mustard seed" faith beginning.

Her life is a parable of inspiring faith and courage and risk for the sake of the gospel of Jesus Christ!

THE PARABLE OF THE TALENTS
READ MATTHEW 25:14–30

Many of Jesus's parables develop his teaching about the kingdom of God, the reign of God that Jesus began through his disciples and early followers. As we have seen, this kingdom contained potential for unlimited growth (like a mustard seed), but that growth may seem to be invisible at first and requires time to grow (like leaven) and eventually it will produce amazing results (the full grown mustard plant with birds resting on it). Through these parables, Jesus was preparing his followers for a ministry which would continue far beyond his

---

9   Lillian Dickson, *These My People: Serving Christ Among the Mountain People of Formosa* (Grand Rapids, MI: Zondervan, 1958), 14.

own departure, like a master who goes away and leaves his estate in the hands of his trusted servants.

In this parable, Jesus lays out a kingdom expectation: we are to invest what he has entrusted into our keeping to expand and grow his kingdom. Each of us has been provided certain gifts and talents, either by birth or experience, which should be used for God's glory.

Jesus describes a master who goes away, leaving behind large amounts of money with his servants. He decided to give differing amounts according to his estimation of their ability.

There is danger with getting too hung up with the seeming inequality of these amounts, but they do point to a reality in life: we all have differing gifts and talents. Please note, though, that no matter what amount these servants invested, the master expected a return from each. Even the servant with just one talent was provided a significant amount of money. Secondly, remember that the money was invested in these servants with the expectation of a return. It wasn't simply a gift to be used for whatever the servant chose.

We must remember, therefore, that we are not responsible for the genetic make-up we are born with, the circumstances of our early lives which have either helped or hindered our discovery of who we are and our strengths and abilities. It would appear from outward appearance that some of us have the equivalent of five talents, others two, and still others one. That would be our judgment. What I hear Jesus telling us in this parable is that everything we have, in terms of natural gifts and abilities, have been given to us by the Provider with a powerful expectation that we will use them to grow that kingdom of God. We've all probably known of individuals with seemingly immense natural gifts who just waste what God has given them.

In this story, however, the focus is upon the one-talent servant who didn't invest what he had; he simply hid it. Perhaps he felt that his investment didn't measure up to the others and felt that it wasn't worth the effort. Here's a "say what" moment for us! I have often met people who, out of a false sense of humility, put themselves down in comparison to others whom we consider to be really talented and gifted. These people fail to use what God has given them.

Douglas Hare, in his commentary, writes,

> It is routine for Christians to excuse themselves by protesting that their gifts are too modest to be significant. This parable insists that the gifts are precious and are to be exploited to the full. "As *each* has received gift, employ it for one another, as good stewards of God's varied grace" (I Peter 4:10).[10]

The difference between the first two and the third servant lies not so much in the amounts entrusted, but that the first two were faithful to exercise the expectation of the master to grow what had been given to them. The third servant gave in to fear and simply buried the investment.

Being safe can be a positive virtue, but it can also be a deterrent to what God desires for us. Many of those who heard this parable for the first time would have felt that the third servant was the most prudent. The first two could indeed have lost some or all of their investment. For the scribes and Pharisees, always at the edges of the crowd, preserving and safeguarding the Jewish faith and law controlled their lives. This hindered them from using their faith to reach out to the broken and wounded people all around them.

Recognize that you will know when you're stretching the borders of your comfort zone by the degree of fear you feel about breaking through into something new and different. Are you willing to take risks to enable a true breakthrough in life? That is a critical element in this parable: the third servant buried his talent out of fear of the master. Surely he must have known of the master's high expectations, just as the other two servants had. For them, however, that expectation challenged them to risk, invest, and bring back a harvest. The third servant's fear drove him in the opposite direction, earning the master's condemnation.

Faith isn't faith unless it is lived. Joy isn't joy unless it is shared. Love isn't love unless it is given away. The final lesson from this parable is that taking risks and investing one's God-given gifts and abilities creates the basis for miraculous growth in the kingdom of God. Like a

---

10 Douglas Hare, *Interpretation: A Bible Commentary for Teach and Preaching—Matthew* (Louisville, KY: John Knox Press, 1993), 288.

mustard seed that must be planted before the life hidden inside it can be released, it is by risking and investing that the kingdom can grow.

Those first two servants took a risk, investing what the master had entrusted them, and they brought back a good return. Their faithfulness was rewarded, and the master entrusted them with far greater responsibilities. They could be trusted to do well with his other properties.

For the third servant, whose fear had led him to inaction, there was to be no reward. This may seem like a harsh verdict, for his portion was given to those who could be trusted to use it better. God is looking for faithful servants in whom he can entrust increasing capacities to grow his kingdom. May you be one of those!

The best way to celebrate what God has given to you is to invest it in serving others, to risk using it as fully as you can. The more you invest, the more it grows. The more you give, the more you receive back. The more you have, the more you can invest to grow the kingdom even more. Planting, reaping, planting again.

Remember the apple seed lesson. The growth potential of God's kingdom is truly unlimited—as long as we are willing to take the risks necessary to continually invest and re-invest what God has given to us!

Living Out Our "Say What" Moment

In this book, we have explored a number of key principles of the kingdom of God taught by Jesus through his parables. The life Jesus offers is like a seed, full of power and potential. Once it's planted, God can produce tremendous growth.

Each one of us resembles such a seed. In creating our individuality, God has placed potential—gifts, abilities, talents—inside each one of us. As we have seen, seeds are potential, but they can also be vulnerable. If sown into dry soil, they may not germinate. They can be choked out by the weeds of cares and circumstances. There is an enemy who sows evil all around, endangering the harvest. For some, however, nothing can stop the growth, like leaven in dough.

At this point, think back to the image of a seed and the necessity of planting them in order for them to germinate and produce growth and an eventual harvest. This chapter has reminded us about the risk we must take to use what God has given us to fulfil the plan he has for us.

Consider your own comfort zone. What are its boundaries? As you get to the edge of your comfort zone, you will experience fear. It's important to confront such fears and doubts. Where have they come from? Are they voices from your past that continue to hinder you? Are they failures that you haven't been able to overcome? Are they doubts about your abilities? Are you putting yourself down by comparing yourself to someone else who you feel has greater faith?

Challenge yourself to stretch the borders of your comfort zone. Where is God directing you to achieve a breakthrough into the new and exciting place he desires for you to be? Can you build your trust in Jesus through the Holy Spirit to enable you to do what at first might seem to be impossible?

Consider the dreams, plans, and visions you may have buried, like the servant in the parable. What might it take to revisit those places? Is God tugging at you to complete something you previously gave up on? Can you revive any dormant gifts that can still be used to grow God's kingdom of love? Is there someone you can turn to for encouragement as you step out of your comfort zone and risk doing something great for God?

Take time to list what God has invested in you. How are you using that investment? Have you produced a return for God, the master? Consider what more God may be asking of you. If you have been faithful so far, what more can God count on you to bring him? Again, challenge your fears and doubts, for God may have something new in mind for you!

Apply these same questions and challenges to your church. What does the comfort zone for your church look like? Where are the borders of anxiety and fear holding your congregation back? Is your church aware of the needs in the community around you, those who are crying out for Jesus's care? What new visions does God have for your church which you need to push through to achieve?

A Prayer for Living Out Our "Say What" Moment

Lord God, you are the God of the miraculous and the seemingly impossible. I rejoice at the stories of great saints who have endured much, risked much, and accomplished much to build your kingdom of love. I also realize that too often my courage has been weak.

Too often I hide inside my comfort zone. I would like to break free of the limitations I have put on my life. I want to be free of the shackles that life and others have imposed on me and which I have accepted too willingly.

Lord, you have a wonderful plan for my life. You have placed gifts and abilities in me to be used to build your kingdom. You are waiting for a return on your investment. I want to live that out. Give me the courage to take the steps necessary to fulfill that plan. Help me to trust that you will protect me. May I hold fast to the vision of Jesus taking my hand, encouraging and challenging me to follow him, as he did with his disciples. Empower me to make a difference for you, Jesus, in my world.

Challenge all the churches of your kingdom, Jesus, to break through the restrictions of fear and worn-out tradition. Break us free of any comfort zones we have allowed to restrict us. Open us to embrace new challenges for you. Give us new visions to accomplish great things for you. In Jesus's name, amen.

Follow Through

Chapter Nine

AT SOME POINT IN OUR LIVES WE'VE ALL MADE VOWS OR NEW YEAR'S resolutions—perhaps too often. We fully intend to keep those promises, but life intervenes and somehow it gets moved to the backburner, discarded in some corner of our minds, or even forgotten altogether. When I clear out some of those back corners of my mind, I discover a number of unfulfilled promises and resolutions. Some were simply unworkable, products of my good imagination. Others, I must admit, turned out to be too difficult to achieve. They remain strong reminders that I should be more careful about what I promise to do.

We all have problems at times with follow through.

I'm reminded of another modern parable I've used in sermons as a reminder about the challenge of follow through, and it'll ring true for anyone who has worked in an organization like a church.

A baseball team once went out to play a regularly scheduled game. The crowd had assembled in the stands, and at the appointed hour the umpire took his rightful place behind home plate and cried out, "Play ball!" As he called out for the first batter to take his place, the catcher for the home team arrived in a rush. Catching his breath, he squatted down behind home plate for the first pitch of the game.

However, looking out into the field, the catcher saw that there was no centre fielder; he later sent his regrets for being unable to get to the game that day, as something had come up. Likewise, there was no third baseman; he had been up too late the night before and needed his rest. The shortstop was in place, but he'd forgotten to bring his glove. Substitute fielders could have been used, but they were all out of town on a weekend trip.

When the pitcher took the mound, he looked around for his teammates. Lo, his heart was heavy, for their places were empty. But the game had been announced, the crowds were in the stands, and the visiting team was in the dugout. The pitcher realized that nothing more could be done. He would have to cover the bases and field the hits.

The inevitable result ensued and the home team lost. But when the absent members of that now defeated team heard about the result of the game, a team meeting was called. The decision was made to secure a new pitcher.

THE TWO SONS
READ MATTHEW 21:25-32

This parable presents a number of "say what" moments. First of all, let's consider the context in which Jesus told this story of two sons. Jesus was teaching in the Temple courts during the week leading up to his arrest and crucifixion. It was a very tense week. The opposition, particularly from the religious authorities, was reaching a critical stage. They had some very serious questions. It was obvious that Jesus spoke with conviction and authority, which challenged their authority. They were troubled by the size of the crowds Jesus attracted and the kind of people who followed him—the poor, the sick, the troubled, and the social outcasts, those who didn't follow the letter of the law. But Jesus commanded their attention and spoke with authority. By whose authority, the Pharisees wondered? That was the question they posed to Jesus.

As was often the case, Jesus didn't provide a direct answer. Instead he asked them by whose authority John the Baptist had taught and baptized. For those religious leaders, this question presented a real problem. If they didn't agree that John had baptised by God's authority, they would antagonize the very people who had experienced a mighty move of God through John's preaching and baptism into new life.

However, these religious authorities who harboured in their heart real doubts about Jesus, desired to trip him up and prove that he hadn't been sent by God. If they admitted that John had had God-given authority to teach and baptize, then Jesus would be able to challenge them on why they didn't accept John's testimony that Jesus was the Messiah, the Son of God.

The authorities simply responded that they didn't know by whose authority Jesus taught. Jesus went on to develop his parable of the two sons.

A father requested that both of his sons work in the family vineyard. Neither son provided an ideal response. The older son agreed to work but didn't show up, much like the baseball players in the modern parable I shared. They made excuses, but the reality is that they just didn't follow through. The younger son initially refused to work, but he later repented and went to work after all. At the end of the story, Jesus raises this question: which son did better? The authorities had to admit that it was the younger son, who had followed through with action.

The key is that one son *did* follow through and the other son *did not*. Jesus was demonstrating that those in the nation's religious circles, like the scribes and Pharisees, strove to maintain their traditions but refused to acknowledge the Messiah in their midst. On the other hand, the tax collectors and sinners lived far outside that Jewish law, but they had responded both to John the Baptist and to Jesus. They had repented of their sin and sought to live lives of the love and grace that had saved them.

This story, unfortunately, brought further condemnation of Jesus by the religious authorities. Like the younger son who initially didn't agree to work but later changed his motivation, it was the common people who responded to Jesus, who did something by repenting and changing their lives. Neither son was ideal, but remember that, for Jesus, the bottom line was a person's decision to follow through with action. He didn't just want pious words; he wanted a changed life.

The challenge for us today is to say yes to Jesus, to pledge to follow him and seek to live a life of loving service. We aren't simply to attend worship and soak in the words of a great preacher, but to head out the door following the service and truly worship the other six days of the week as disciples and apostles of the love of Jesus.

Commentator Douglas Hare acknowledges the original context of this controversy with the religious authorities, but he points out that it probably has a wider application. We, too, can fall into the trap of those authorities, having good intentions but poor follow through:

> Christians too, can become blind to what God is doing in the world around them. How easily "church work" degenerates into little more than simply maintaining the institution, with no excitement concerning what God's active grace is doing and consequently no enthusiasm for evangelism and renewal! We say that we are going to work in the vineyard but instead of harvesting the grapes we spend our time rearranging the stones along the path![11]

THE TWO HOUSE-BUILDERS
READ MATTHEW 7:24-27, LUKE 6:46-49

Jesus concludes his Sermon on the Mount with the parable of the two house-builders. In this simple story, Jesus contrasts two men. It would appear that their houses were similarly constructed. Both houses, once finished, were expected to stand firm against storms or calamities. However, one man built his home on a solid foundation, anchored to the bedrock; he was wise, taking the extra time and effort to build a lasting home. The second man was foolish, building his house on flat, sandy soil.

Those listening to Jesus must have felt that the sandy soil represented the holy land's riverbeds, which remained dry most of the year. Such soil would seem inviting, as the builder wouldn't need to go to the extra effort and expense of digging deep into the rock. But the reality of these flat river valleys was that occasionally storms came and they filled up quickly with floodwater.

---

11 Douglas Hare, *Matthew*, 93.

When my wife and I visited Israel a few years ago, we experienced such storms. In fact, they delayed our landing. It was fascinating to see the hillsides suddenly turn green from the moisture. At one point we saw a stream flowing over a roadway. The rains came so fast that the water didn't soak in; it ran off into these flooding river valleys.

When the storms came, in the parable, only the secure house, built carefully on bedrock, stood firm. The one built by the foolish builder was swept away.

Jesus told this story to demonstrate the importance of follow through. He expected people to not only hear his words, but to follow through by acting on them. Simply listening and being impressed by his teachings wasn't sufficient. If those teachings didn't change a person's life, they wouldn't be equipped to deal with the storms of life when they came. Remember: the storms struck both houses, but only one survived. In Jesus's illustration, the wise builder both heard his teachings and applied them, living them out.

I see a warning here. To become true disciples of Jesus, we must take all the teachings of Jesus, such as the Sermon on the Mount, and allow them to transform our lives. This is demanding. For example, Jesus references the commandment against murder, but he goes further to warn us about nursing anger in our hearts, which can later lead to murder or the dissolution of a relationship. We are to love those who hurt us, pray for our enemies, and resist hate. We are to resist the temptation to find fault in others while ignoring the same faults in ourselves. Blessed are we when we become peacemakers, when we mourn, even when we may be persecuted for our faith.

Note that the word discipleship comes from the same root word as discipline. This will help enable us to follow through our professions with action.

The man who built his house on the sandy soil chose the quick and easy solution. Too often, so do we. The foolish man didn't take into consideration what might occur in the future, blissfully ignoring the realities of potential weather his house could not withstand. By not exercising discipline to strengthen our lives and keep us secure on the bedrock of faith in Jesus, we run the same risk. Storms will come. Floods will rise to threaten us. The winds of circumstances can be strong enough to blow us off course.

Fred Craddock has pointed out that the confession of Jesus as Lord,

> no matter how exuberant, when unaccompanied by obedience will not hold one's life when the storms hit. It is in the storms, and the faithful seem to face more of them than anyone else, that the difference between interested listeners and obedient disciples will be evident.[12]

I invite you to read, or reread, the words of life given by Jesus in the Sermon on the Mount (Matthew 5–7). Then make sure you're not just hearing inspiration but taking action in your life. Wise are those who both hear and follow through with doing the words of Jesus.

Living Out Our "Say What" Moment

Go back through your life and remember some of the promises, vows, and resolutions you have made. Then check them over. How many have you been able to fulfill? Probably not as many as you'd like. That's okay, for we all have a long list of unrealized promises which accumulate over time. Have you been too quick to promise something, offer help, take on a position, or change a habit? What kind of rationalizations or excuses have you made for failing to follow through?

Out of that list, allow yourself to let go of items that perhaps you never really intended to follow through on, the ones that don't really matter. On the other hand, take a serious look at the promises you have broken and the pledges you've left unrealized. Are there any that you can revisit in a serious way, to renew your vow or redirect your promise? Prayerfully seek God's wisdom. Ask him to give you the strength to fulfill that vow or rededicate yourself to the promise you made to another. Seek forgiveness for anyone to whom you made a promise and did not follow through with action.

---

12 Craddock, *Luke*, 93.

We all face the temptation to be too careless with our words, and certainly that is borne out in our culture today. Promises seem cheap and far too easily backed off from. Yet some of those promises—like marriage vows, accepting Jesus as Lord and Saviour, or pledging to raise a child in the Christian faith—are crucial. Ask God to guard the words you speak. Seek his strength to ensure that your yes means yes and your no means no. Strive to be a person of integrity whom others can trust.

Jesus desires for our words to be reflected in our actions. We must not only hear the Word, but also do the Word. Check your faith life: is it built on the solid rock of the life and teachings of Jesus, or are you allowing yourself to take the easy way of building on the shifting sands of culture? How might you better anchor yourself to Jesus? In what ways might you truly live out your faith day by day?

A Prayer for Living Out Our "Say What" Moment

Lord God, I have reviewed my life and discovered many unfulfilled promises and unkept vows. Perhaps in doing this I have caused hurt in my relationships. Perhaps I have let you down by failing to follow through in faith. Forgive me, Lord. Enable me to seek forgiveness from anyone I may have let down. Give me the courage to look at the vows and promises I have made, and then strengthen me to truly follow through. Guard my tongue from making promises I cannot or will not fulfill. Enable me to be a person of integrity so others can trust what I promise them.

Lord, I desire to serve you with all my life. Strengthen me when I am tempted to take the easier path of just getting along in life, of going with the flow of culture, of not taking the time to build a firm relationship with you. May I build the house of my faith on the solid rock of Jesus and his teachings. May I discover ways of living out that faith day by day in all the situations and circumstances I find myself in. May my actions and words always be one and the same. In Jesus's name, amen.

Humility

Chapter Ten

How many of you have been to summer camp? For many years, my wife, daughter, and I attended a family music camp. For one week we enjoyed all kinds of music, Bible studies, worship times, and campfires. Plus, we were part of all the fun and foolishness of camp. You may also remember the watchful eyes at mealtimes looking out for anyone who could be caught with their elbows on the table. Once caught, you were required to do things like run around the dining hall—or, since this was a music camp, stand up on your chair and sing.

Some of us discovered that if you sang a really "bad" song, you wouldn't be challenged again. One song I came up with was a satirical song written years ago by Mac Davis, entitled "Oh Lord, It's Hard to be Humble." The chorus speaks of the struggle of staying humble when you know you're perfect in every way. You get the drift.

The song comes back to me when I reflect upon the Christian virtue of humility. We like to poke fun at the pompous, the arrogant, and the vain who parade before us. We've already met some very self-absorbed individuals in the parables, such as that rich fool who prided himself on his wealth and wanted to build bigger barns rather than share his abundance—that is, until he suddenly died and left it all behind.

As we read through the gospels, we find that Jesus was often opposed by the Pharisees. He spoke many of his parables in the context of this tension with the religious authorities. We often view Pharisees as caricatures of pompous, pride-filled, arrogant, and self-righteous individuals. But then, what is humility?

THE PHARISEE AND THE PUBLICAN
READ LUKE 18:9–14

In this parable of the Pharisee and the publican, we meet such a Pharisee, one whom we could too easily write off. This parable produced a very powerful "say what" reaction from those who originally heard it.

First of all, allow me to give some credit to the Pharisees. I believe Jesus had a real heart for these diligent defenders of the Jewish faith, and his confrontations with them were birthed from concern. At the time, members of the Pharisee branch of Judaism were highly respected and strove to faithfully and sacrificially live out the Torah and the holy traditions of the Jewish faith. The Pharisee in this parable would have been a highly moral person, living as pure a life as he could in light of the law. In his prayer, he indicates that he tithed and fasted twice a week, which went beyond the requirements of the law. This Pharisee also attended prayer and worship at the Temple, where he lifted up his prayers in this story. We will return to this Pharisee in a moment.

Now, let us consider the publican. Publicans were tax collectors who were despised by most of Jewish society. The people of Israel resented having their country occupied by Rome. However, some Jewish people collaborated with Rome to become collectors of the taxes that Rome imposed on the country. Rome was only interested in receiving what was allocated, so a tax collector had free rein to collect as much as he could and pocket the difference. Therefore, Jewish tax collectors were considered to be both traitors and extortionists. Due to this, it would have been highly unusual for a publican to be at prayer in the Temple. The Pharisee would have had to keep his distance from the publican in order not to be defiled. However, in this parable we discover a publican in earnest prayer to God just steps away from the praying Pharisee.

Two men, two prayers. Then comes the "say what" moment, for Jesus indicates that only one of them went home justified and blessed by God—and it turns out not to be the respectful and respected Pharisee, but rather the despised publican. Say what? What gives? Why does Jesus commend only the publican?

Let us consider the prayer of the Pharisee. Remember not to write him off as a self-righteous, prideful soul, but we do need to unpack some critical elements of the prayer. The most serious issue is that his prayer wasn't really directed to God; rather, it was a recitation of all the wonderful things the Pharisee felt he had accomplished in his defence of the faith. Note how many times he used the pronoun "I." His righteousness was based entirely on his own efforts.

As we consider the virtue of humility in this chapter, we need to analyze this Pharisee using the concept of narcissism. This is the human tendency towards self-absorption, the egotistical admiration of one's own attributes. The term comes from Greek mythology, in which the character Narcissus was captivated by his own reflection in a pond.

While researching this condition, I found that it operates on a sliding scale from the kind of selfishness we all indulge in at times to extreme psychopathic behaviours. Narcissism has the following characteristics:

- An obvious self-focus in relationships, demanding attention from others.
- A lack of empathy to the needs and feelings of others.
- An inflated sense of self-importance and feeling of entitlement.
- A hypersensitivity to criticism.
- A lack of thankfulness or gratitude.
- Delusional thinking, usually centred around oneself and one's sense of importance.

It's intriguing to look at the Pharisee along these lines. He certainly had a sense of entitlement due to his religious position, with a feeling of smug superiority. His prayer indicated a sense of self-focus (remember all the "I" pronouns), and he showed no thanks or gratitude to God for what he had received. Instead his prayer was all about what he had done for God. He didn't demonstrate any need for God. Sadly, he lacked any empathy for the publican, basically rejecting the publican and his reason for being at the Temple in need of God.

Jesus recognized our all too human temptation to be self-focused and self-centred. One of the reasons for our current concern about narcissism is that our culture encourages a me-first orientation, leading us to base our lives on our wants rather than our needs, to want things to go our own way. The Pharisee demonstrated all of this, but he also tied his pride of self to his spirituality, resulting in the self-righteousness that Jesus rejects.

It would be well for us to consider just where along that narcissism scale we lie. Are our prayers just recitations of our worthiness before God, or do we seek him as a child would cry out to a loving parent?

In the parable, the publican is the one who cries out in just that way to God. Commentators have wondered about why the publican turned up at the Temple to pray that day, considering his outcast status in Jewish society. Certainly those religious officials hearing the story would have been astonished that Jesus was justifying the publican, saying that his prayers were heard whereas the hyper-religious Pharisee's prayers were not.

THE STORY OF ZACCHAEUS
READ LUKE 19:1-10

We can perhaps glimpse some of the publican's motivation by turning to the story of Zacchaeus, who was a tax-collecting publican much like the one in the parable. When Jesus entered Jericho, Zacchaeus was up in a tree, desiring to catch at least a glimpse of Jesus as he passed by. Surprise, surprise; Jesus looked up, called Zacchaeus down, and invited himself to lunch with him.

Say what? Jesus bypassed the seemingly important people of Jericho to dine with a rejected sinner. But then, Jesus must have sensed what was in Zacchaeus's heart: a desire to turn away from a life of cheating people out of their money, of paying back what had formerly been dishonestly gained.

Perhaps a similar motivation existed with the publican in the parable. Perhaps he, too, had experienced a change of heart and was crying out to God for forgiveness and healing of his spirit as he desired to begin a new life. The publican's prayer was honest and from the heart. In this sense, he truly exhibited humility.

For me, humility comes from making an honest assessment of who we are and *whose* we are. When we recognize that all that we are and have comes ultimately from Creator God, we will develop a proper sense of our own self, our own *God-given* gifts and abilities, and a deep gratitude to God for them.

I fear that we sometimes make a caricature of this Publican, too, picturing a person who pounds his chest and cries out, "Lord, I'm so unworthy!" That's false humility. Each one of us is a unique, beloved creation of God. Into each of us he has given special gifts and talents. For the publican, this may have included his capacity for money and finances. It could have been valuable to God for him to use these skills for God's glory rather than building his own wealth.

A true sense of humility lies not in putting ourselves down or fearing pride, but in celebrating our God-given talents. It shouldn't be too hard to be humble in this way, which will create a true and more secure sense of self than the propped-up narcissism exhibited by the Pharisee. When we can acknowledge our own God-given uniqueness, we will be in a position to celebrate the uniqueness of everyone else.

There may be some who still feel a sense of judgment, whether it's judged by themselves, by others, or by God, about who they've been in life and what sins they've committed. Humility in no way enables condemnation. If you've accepted the loving forgiveness of Jesus, you become a new person, a new creation in Jesus (2 Corinthians 5:16–21). The past is washed away and you must resist any negative aspect of that past creeping back into your life. That may be who you *were*, but it certainly isn't who you *are*. Celebrate that you are now a new person in Jesus. Embrace the flow of the power of the Holy Spirit enabling your new life in Jesus to flourish.

True humility frees us from the need to compare ourselves to others. Jesus frees us from any thoughts of looking down on those we consider lesser to build our own ego or put ourselves down by comparing ourselves to those we consider to be more wealthy or more successful.

True humility is the foundation for community and the essential glue of the church. Consider the wonderful image of the church developed by St. Paul as the body of Christ (Romans 12, 1 Corinthians 12). Jesus is alive in our fellowship as we embrace each other's unique gifts. Realize that all gifts are essential and none is superior. We must resist our human temptation to compare ourselves to one another. There is no place for narcissistic pride or arrogance. Neither is there a place for anyone feeling worthless. As we each discover our special place in that amazing body, we can truly become brothers and sisters in Christ!

Living Out Our "Say What" Moment

Check yourself. You may not feel that you're as arrogant or self-righteous as the Pharisee in the parable, but think about how often you use the pronoun "I" in your conversations. How many times do you wait for a chance to talk about yourself? How important do you feel yourself to be? Consider the concept of entitlement: do you feel that you need more recognition because of what you've done or accomplished in your life? In your prayers, do you seek to build a loving relationship with God, or are you guilty, like the Pharisee, of parading your good deeds and great spirituality before God?

On the other hand, are you too quick to put yourself down, feeling that this means you are humble before God? Remember that when you came to Jesus, he made you a new creation. This book emphasizes the teachings of Jesus regarding accepting ourselves as a gift of creation, of the power and potential God has placed within us. Too often we restrict ourselves. Remember that true humility means recognizing who we each are in the sight of God. True humility gives God glory for the unique gifts and abilities within each of us. When we are truly humble, we never put ourselves down; rather, we glorify God in celebrating and then applying what God has given us.

Now, evaluate your humility: can you make a true reckoning of yourself as seen through the eyes of Jesus? How might that vision change your view of yourself and your place in the kingdom of God?

Consider how easily you can celebrate the uniqueness and gifts of others. The Pharisee glorified himself by falsely comparing himself with the publican. We too often do that. Perhaps at times we feel smugly superior to others whom we feel have made a mess of their lives. Resist any temptation to compare yourself to others. Each one of us is unique.

In what ways can you encourage and support those around you to discover and accept who they are in Jesus? In what ways can you celebrate their unique gifts? How can we use this perspective on humility to truly build up the kingdom of God in our churches?

A Prayer for Living Out Our "Say What" Moment

Loving God, I rejoice in your creation of my unique self. I praise you for the personality, gifts, talents, and dreams that you have placed within me. I give thanks that I am your child whom you deeply care for. I admit that there are times when I'm focused more on myself than on you or others. I like to have things go my way. I crave recognition from others for what I do. I realize that at times I have cared more about myself, and that has hindered me from realizing the needs and sufferings of others. Forgive me when I'm self-centred, when I've looked down on others so I can feel better than they are.

Lord, I also realize that I have entertained false humility, putting myself down. I have compared myself to those whom I feel have superior gifts or firmer faith, and that has prevented me from using all that you have given me. Grant to me true humility so that I can see in myself the gift you have created and then properly use what you have given me to serve Jesus. Grant to me true humility so that when I look at others I don't see someone who's inferior or superior but rather a unique person to be encouraged and celebrated.

Build up your people, O Lord, in the love of Jesus who with God's humility ministers to each and every one of us whose lives touch his. In Jesus's name, amen.

Judgment

Chapter Eleven

I WOULD LIKE YOU TO CONSIDER TWO IMAGES: A WINDOW AND A MIRROR.

First of all, let's think about the window. Imagine a window looking out upon the world. This represents the way you view the world around you. How large is this window in your life? Is it large enough to take in all that lies out there, or have you narrowed your vista?

Think about those things that can shrink down your window on the world. Consider aspects of your life that influence your vision. For example, your background can include prejudices. The conditioning brought about by your upbringing can influence you. Your life experiences can also influence your thinking, and the opinions of others around you may shape how you perceive things. Without being aware of it, our window on the world can be limited and we see what we want to see. We don't realize how small our window may be.

This is a way of visualizing *what we see of the world around us.*

How clear is the glass through which you're looking? As well as having a small window, the view itself can be obscured. It can be smudged by past life experiences, failures, and harsh judgments passed upon us that we've internalized. It can be darkened by discouragement and depression. It can be clouded by illness, loss, or suffering, which of course limits what we're able to take in. You may have tried hard to keep the glass clear, but situations and circumstances keep blocking the view.

This is a way of visualizing *how we see the world around us.*

We will return to the image of a window as we study this chapter's parable, but first let us turn to our second image: the mirror. A mirror is a way of visualizing *how we see ourselves.*

When we gaze into the mirror, what do we truly see? We may not like what we see: a less than ideal face to take out into public, a fear that others will judge us as being less than attractive, or despair about how to acquire the clear, youthful faces we see on magazine covers. As we gaze into our mirror, are we willing or able to see and accept ourselves as we really are?

Think of your mirror as reflecting not just your physical face but your soul. How well is that soul? Do you see a valuable child of God or a wounded human being? Are you able to appreciate your whole self, all the good and all the not so wonderful? Can you risk being totally honest as you gaze upon your image? How is your relationship with God in Jesus? What is the state of your spiritual life? Is it glowing from the face in the mirror? Or do you see someone struggling with doubts and fears? Can you sense a loving God looking through the mirror at you and appreciating what he sees—a unique child of God born with the purpose of building his kingdom of peace and love? Or do you harbour a sense of self judgment as you stare into your mirror?

THE ENEMY'S CROP
READ MATTHEW 13:24-30

We've already seen that Jesus often used the themes of planting and harvesting in his parables, images that would have been quite familiar to the people of Israel. This parable begins again with sowing seed, but then it takes an unusual twist.

A farmer carefully sowed his crop of wheat. He did everything correctly. However, on the night after he sowed his crop, an enemy snuck in and planted a second crop alongside the wheat. This second crop consisted of a weed called bearded darnel, a poisonous rye-grass which was very common. In the early stages of growth, it's practically impossible to distinguish from wheat. As soon as the grain matured, though, the difference was obvious. By that time, the wheat and darnel had grown so closely together that it was impossible to remove the weeds without destroying the wheat as well. They had to be harvested together and then the grain needed to be separated.

This is a parable about judgment. First of all, the farmer looked out upon a reality that included both good and evil. An enemy has sown a crop of weeds, potentially destroying his wheat. For the disciples of Jesus, they too were grappling with the reality that the forces of evil were present all around them. In fact, those forces were pressing in upon Jesus more and more every day. The harvest looked pretty mixed-up.

Please note this reality of evil as you look out upon an often depressingly evil and mixed-up world. This parable acknowledges the presence of evil and the enemy, satan, who's behind it all. Evil was facing Jesus, and despite the victory of the cross and empty tomb, we still face evil in the present age. Do we pull the shutters and give up? No. In the parable, the farmer allowed the crop to continue to grow. Despite what he saw when he looked out at his crop, despite the evil seed planted by the enemy, the crop had to keep maturing until harvest time.

This enables us to maintain our window into the world with a sense of hope. Despite the invasion of weeds, the crop will be harvested and the weeds winnowed out. The good grain will survive. A strong lesson in this story is that no matter how discouraging it may be to constantly face evil, discouragement, and disappointment, the powerful seed of God's kingdom will grow and flourish, even side by side with the evil seeds. Our vision requires the lens of hope to see the good seed that's growing out there beyond our windows.

The next step in grappling with this parable is to consider the reaction of the farmer's servants. They wanted to step in and pull out all the weeds that had sprouted up alongside the wheat. At times we may get upset at the evil we see around us, and it's tempting to desire to step in and eradicate it. The disciples would have liked God to more directly intervene against the opposition they and Jesus faced every day. At one point, they wanted Jesus to consider calling down fire from heaven to wipe out those enemies (Luke 9:52).

Jesus resisted those disciples' request, as did the farmer reject the suggestions of his servants. No, the wheat and darnel had to keep growing together until the eventual harvest. If they attempted to pull out the weeds, they could also pull up of the valuable wheat.

This is a lesson on making judgments. Too often, we as Christians feel that those people whom we've judged to be "weeds" need to be severely dealt with. In the process, more harm than good is accomplished. Perhaps we've all felt this way about dealing with the opposition, wondering, "Why can't God just take that person away?" Remember that Jesus has instructed us not to react in anger to those who oppose us, but rather to pray for anyone we would consider an enemy.

THE SPECK AND THE LOG
READ MATTHEW 7:1-5

In this segment of Jesus's Sermon the Mount, we find a strong teaching about making judgments about other people. Here, Jesus is dealing with a situation similar to the servants who wanted to rip out the weeds. The servants could eventually tell what was good and what the enemy had planted, but the farmer had to first counsel them against taking immediate action against the weeds, which would have produced more harm than good.

This doesn't mean we are prohibited from discernment. Far from it; discernment is a critical spiritual element in our lives. Jesus strongly admonishes us not to judge. We often rush to judgment about another person and find them wanting on some level, based on outward appearances which can be very deceiving.

Now let's return to our mirror example. When we beam out a critical spirit at others, it often masks our own inability to truly gaze honesty into the mirror and accept our faults. Jesus puts it strongly: why get so worked up about pointing out the speck in another person's eye while ignoring the log taking up space in our own eye? By the same measure as we judge others, we will be judged.

St. Paul reminds us that God, not us, is ultimately in charge. We are not to be overcome by evil but to overcome evil with good (Romans 12:16–21). This means that it is our responsibility to ensure that the good seed keeps growing, even while the weeds are growing, much as may dislike that reality. In that way, there will be a harvest. It will be up to God to sort it all out in the end.

We are called to be salt and light in a world that can appear pretty dark at times. Evil is still growing all around us. It's not our job to root out those we don't approve of. Our job is to love as Jesus loves, seeking for us to forgive and pray for our enemies. Are we able to look into the mirror and perceive any logs that are lurking there? Are we then willing to deal with those logs and loose ourselves from criticizing and judging the perceived faults in others?

This is ultimately both a parable of judgment and of trust. God will triumph over evil. A rich harvest will take place. Sifting and sorting will occur. Good will be vindicated and evil dealt with. For the time being, we are called to be faithful to God, following the loving and grace-filled pathway of Jesus our Lord.

I would like to add one point to this parable. In maintaining the health of our growing seed and ceasing to be critical and judgmental of others, we have the opportunity to actually change weeds into wheat. We can be an example and an encouragement, enabling others to gaze into the mirror of their lives. We can support them to clear their vision with the reality that the God who looks through the mirror at them loves them, accepts them, and has a wonderful plan for the rest of their lives. Jesus invites us to participate in changing weeds into fruitful wheat so that the harvest may be bountiful and full! The best way to deal with an enemy is to turn that individual into a friend in Jesus!

Living Out Our "Say What" Moment

Let us return to the image of the window. You've had a chance to think about how you look out at your world. How wide or narrow is that window? Have you, even unconsciously, blocked out some of that world? It is difficult, I realize, to take in all the evil, pain, and suffering that's going on out there. It's challenging to see the negative forces growing up, like those weeds in the parable, alongside everything good. But we need to keep our eyes open to the world. Someone once said that if you read the newspaper, you should do it with prayer. I think that goes with TV, the internet, and the whole range of technology that brings the world into our hands. So, pray for the world.

We also considered the nature of the glass in your window. The glass you're looking through will influence how you perceive your world and the people in it. Check yourself again: what kind of judgments do you make based on that filter? What categories do you place people in due to their appearance or race or clothing? Do you see just another street person or a child of God who has suffered much? Are there any people or groups of people you might want to write off? Have you at times wished that God would bring fire from heaven upon those who oppose you, like the disciples of Jesus wished?

Take a look through the life and ministry of Jesus. He didn't refuse to talk to a Samaritan woman at the well just because of her ethnicity. He reached out to touch a leper even though that individual was considered unclean. He forgave a woman who had been caught in the act of adultery and saved her life from those who had judged her a sinner and were prepared to stone her to death. May we all live like Jesus.

Now, let us turn back to the mirror. In the parable, Jesus warned us against making hasty judgments. We are to allow God to be the final arbiter of what is good and evil. We reviewed some stern teaching from Jesus in his Sermon on the Mount about making judgments. He identified the all too common human tendency to judge others while ignoring our own weaknesses and problems. We pick away at the faults of others while ignoring those we harbour inside.

So let us take a good look in the mirror. What do you see? What areas of your life need some attention? What weaknesses need a dose of the Holy Spirit? What bad habits have you been holding onto that need to be broken? That which you find annoying in others may be a sign of a problem in yourself. If you do some internal housecleaning, you'll probably find that you become more sensitive to the struggles of others and less tempted to find fault in them.

As Christians, we are to become like Jesus as he lives in us. This means that when we look out at the world, we do it with the eyes of Jesus. Think about the window through which you see your world. How can that view become more Christ-like? Can you look at others as Jesus did, as precious children of the heavenly Father, some of whom need care, healing, and compassion? Are there areas of brokenness out there that call us to be peacemakers and healers? How might you be light and salt in the community around you?

As you look into the mirror, enable yourself to see Jesus looking back at you. One crucial aspect of coming to faith in Jesus Christ is being able to see ourselves as Jesus in the Word sees us: of great value to him and his kingdom. So often in Jesus's parable, we see that the kingdom of God is built person by person, seed by seed. Consider how important each of us is in the great plan to spread the gospel of love deed by deed. Consider that Jesus is looking upon you with the great love and compassion he showed everyone in his life. Feel him not condemning you for any of your faults, but desiring you to be free from old wounds and anything that hinders your partnership with him in ministry. See yourself as a living embodiment of Jesus. Then open your window and door and step outside to serve him with energy and joy!

A Prayer for Living Out Our "Say What" Moment

Lord God, I realize that I look out on my world with some limitations. There are things I don't like and don't want to see. Sometimes I allow prejudices and other people's opinions cloud my vision. Lord, this is your world. I understand from Scripture that evil exists side by side everything you desire. At times I would like all that evil to be destroyed, but comfort me with the knowledge that ultimately you will sort it all out.

Lord, enable me not to make hasty judgments about others. Help me to see the precious people they are and not be swayed by how they dress or the colour of their skin. Lord, enable me to take a deep look in the mirror, particularly before I cast a judgment on someone else. May I see clearly any faults that I have allowed into my life, bad habits I haven't overcome, or anything that could block the full and abundant life you desire for me to live. Forgive and heal me.

In looking out at my world, may I have your vision, seeing with compassion and love and not judgment. In looking at myself, may I see Jesus seeing me with eyes of care, willing me to accept him more deeply and live for him more fully. Lead me out into the world to transform lives with the love and grace of Jesus. In Jesus's name, amen.

Mercy

Chapter Twelve

IN 2007, MY WIFE LORRAINE AND I WERE PRIVILEGED TO EXPERIENCE A brief tour of Israel and explore many of the places mentioned in the Bible. Walking the steps of Jerusalem and sailing the waters of Galilee provided some wonderful experiences. Although it was just a taste, we truly desire to return for much more. The Bible comes alive when you're in the exact places where events recorded in Scripture took place.

We stayed for two nights on the shores of Galilee and explored that region. We then travelled south along the Jordan River, stopping at Ein Gedi, Qumron, and Masada before arriving for the night at a hotel by the Dead Sea. That trip takes you through many different ecological zones as you descend in elevation, for the Dead Sea is one of the lowest places on earth, far below sea level. Leaving the lush semitropical shores of Galilee, the land becomes increasingly arid as you travel south. The Jordan River, too, grows smaller and smaller as you approach the Dead Sea, as so much water is diverted from its flow for agriculture.

But there is another dramatic dynamic going on with the two seas, Galilee and Dead. The Sea of Galilee receives water from Mount Hermon in the north of Israel, a snow-covered peak. Galilee's waters then empty into the Jordan River and ultimately flow into the Dead Sea. However, the Dead Sea is named for the fact that it receives water but has no outflow. The water remains there, eventually evaporating and leaving behind salt and mineral content, which means that you more float than swim in that body of water.

This provides a great teaching illustration about mercy. Mercy exists in both receiving and giving, like the Sea of Galilee. The health of the Sea of Galilee exists in the fact that it both receives and gives water. Our spiritual health exists in our ability to not only receive from God, but also to give back and share his love with others. An unforgiving spirit and denial of mercy blocks up life, creating stagnation, as in the Dead Sea. If you block the flow of God's love, if you receive God's love but refuse to share that love, your life will dry up.

Galilee is rich in fish and surrounded by green hills and lush vegetation. Nothing—no fish, no seaweed—exists in the Dead Sea.

THE UNMERCIFUL SERVANT
READ MATTHEW 18:21-35

Simon Peter came to Jesus with a question, asking how many times he should extend forgiveness to a brother when he sinned against him. Peter went on to offer more than the expected three times, by going up to seven. Jesus gave Peter and all those listening a truly "say what" response: forgive seventy times seven! That is a staggering amount and basically means extending forgiveness far beyond the realm of calculation. The real issue for Jesus was not "how much and how often," but rather the reality that mercy and forgiveness are absolute essentials for living out the kingdom of God.

He follows that teaching with this parable on the unmerciful servant.

A king, seeking to settle accounts with his servants, discovered that one of them owed him ten thousand talents. This would have represented a staggering amount of money in Jesus's day, something like ten million dollars in today's terms. It was a deliberate exaggeration by Jesus to catch the attention of those hearing it, making the story more dynamic. Remember, these parables were told to make a strong point. It would be unthinkable for the servant to be able to pay back such a sum, so the king ordered the servant and his family to be sold so that some repayment could be made. This would only pay back a pittance of what was owed.

Still, the servant begged for time to repay. Again, this must have evoked a strong reaction as it would have taken several lifetimes to return this huge amount. The servant must have somehow embezzled much of the king's wealth and estate to have incurred such a vast debt. The king, though, showed mercy on this servant and simply wiped out the debt. The servant was forgiven and free to go. This would have struck the hearers of the parable as very odd indeed; wiping out such a vast debt represented a huge sacrifice on the part of the king.

Following his merciful release, the servant encountered a fellow servant. It turned out that this second servant owed him a small debt of a hundred denari. A denari was roughly a day's wages. You might think that this servant, filled with a sense of immense relief at the mercy he had received, would express his gratitude by forgiving the second servant's debt. But no, he demanded repayment of the small sum. The second servant also begged for mercy, insisting that he would repay it. The first servant, however, unmercifully denied him his request and had him thrown into prison.

You may have been hurt by another person and feel entitled to seek some form of retribution. You may have caused hurt to someone else, and they might have the power to seek retribution from you. The king in the parable had full right to demand repayment, and even sell the servant and all his possessions, if necessary, to pay back a small part of the debt.

However, another dynamic comes into play through this parable: mercy. If you have the power to demand retribution, or someone else has that power over you to demand retribution, and it is not used, that is mercy. When someone has mercy on you, it means you don't get what you deserve. What we deserve is justice; being forgiven is mercy—and this parable is a great example of mercy.

The amount of debt owed by the first servant in the parable could never be paid back. The essence of the forgiveness offered to us through the sacrifice of Jesus is such an amount that no human could ever repay. Jesus paid a debt that we could never repay: *"But by the free gift of God's grace all are put right with him through Christ Jesus, who sets them free"* (Romans 3:24).

A second dynamic lies in the reaction of the first servant to the mercy offered by the king. He demonstrated no gratitude, probably thinking that he had gotten away with it.

The true test of receiving lies in our gratitude for the mercy that has been given to us. The ingratitude of the unmerciful servant was manifested in his unwillingness to extend even a small bit of mercy to his fellow servant. This is what brought the severe reaction of anger from the king, and the eventual condemnation of that first servant, who was handed over to the king's torturers.

The same applies to us. Are we as willing to mercifully forgive as we have been forgiven? The unmerciful servant was eventually imprisoned. Holding on to bitterness and being unwilling to forgive can be like imprisoning ourselves. Someone once said that the world's darkest prison is that of an unforgiving heart. The outward flow of mercy is essential to the life Jesus offers, but it requires us to extend the loving forgiveness of Jesus. We receive love and forgiveness from God but must return the gift through our own loving actions. By doing so, we can receive even more of the blessings of God into our lives.

As we recite the Lord's Prayer, with its refrain for us to forgive as we are forgiven, we can avoid becoming like the Dead Sea, only receiving and drying up in the process. The Christian life must demonstrate the flow of the Holy Spirit! When you forgive someone, you don't allow what has happened to stand between you. There is a potential for broken relationships to be restored. Even if that may not be possible, if that other person is unwilling to repent, we can rid our hearts of bitterness and the desire for retribution, which can destroy our lives.

Reconciliation requires both parties to be merciful. Paul, in Romans 12:18, reminds us that we are to live at peace with everyone as far as it is possible for us. Sadly, there are people with whom it is not possible for us to live at peace. They reject any and all sincere efforts at reconciliation. But go ahead and forgive them anyway and move on. Forgiveness doesn't wipe out what has happened, magically make it right, or eliminate the natural consequences that result from it. Mercy, given through faith in our merciful Saviour, can free us. We have the opportunity to constantly lift up that person to God in prayer, praying that their heart would be softened to receive the mercy God holds for them. We must maintain that flow of mercy through our lives, receiving God's merciful forgiveness in Jesus, giving out that same merciful love into our world, and receiving even more of God's love in the process!

Living Out Our "Say What" Moment

God is merciful and eager to forgive and restore each of his children to a deep loving relationship. This is emphasized again and again in the teaching ministry of Jesus, and particularly in these parables.

Picture for yourself that loving father racing out to greet the return of his wayward son, not even taking time to hear the son's speech of contrition, and restoring him to full status in the family. That is our merciful God who in Jesus has paid the penalty for our sin, forgiven us, and restored us to full relationship with him.

Have you truly received all of God's grace-filled mercy? Are there any old wounds that you're still clinging to? Do you have any pain still buried deep inside? Is it difficult for you to fully let go of the guilt that has built up over the years from things you've said or done? In coming to Jesus, you become a new creation with all your past wounds, guilt, sin, and pain washed away (2 Corinthians 5:17). Therefore, let it all go. Forgive yourself! Let God take it all and instead put a robe on you! God is merciful all the time!

Check your ability and willingness to extend that same mercy to everyone in your life. Be watchful for the danger of your rational self, which can cause you to entertain thoughts of entitlement, anger, and retribution against those who have hurt you. Remember that biblical mercy means giving up on your felt need for justice. Remember also that the hurts we harbour deep in our hearts when we are unwilling to forgive often cause us more suffering than the person who has harmed us. If you often go over old grievances and wounds, bitterness can develop that causes great harm to you both spiritually and physically.

So, who do you need to forgive? From whom do you need to seek forgiveness?

When you feel you have done all you can to extend mercy in order to seek the restoration of a relationship, you can do more, even if the person does not accept. In prayer, give the situation to God. Be persistent in prayer for that person, praying that God will bring about a softening of their spirit and an acceptance of His forgiveness. We are called by Jesus to pray for any who have used us in a negative way, to pray for anyone who appears to be an enemy.

A Prayer for Living Out Our "Say What" Moment

Lord God, I come to you, seeking to fully comprehend what you have given to me by Jesus on the cross. He took all my sin and pain and weakness. May I be like that younger son, surprised by the immensity of grace from a loving Father who desires me to live in the deepest and most loving relationship with him. I confess that I still rehearse old wounds, hurts, and pain that others have caused me. In my heart lurks old guilt from things I have said and done that have caused hurt.

Thank you for making me a new person in Jesus, free to live and love. In the power of your Holy Spirit, enable me to be as merciful to others as you have been to me. Empower me to let go of the need to get even with anyone who has hurt me. Give me patience to keep praying for that person and keep me persistent in praying for them, even if they don't accept my offer of forgiveness. May we all truly receive and give by your Spirit, unlike the dry and lifeless Dead Sea. Merciful Jesus, we are so thankful for your grace. Amen.

Compassion

Chapter Thirteen

OUR MISSION TEAM GATHERED FOR MORNING WORSHIP ON THE PATIO OF Angel's Inn on the outskirts of Managua, Nicaragua. We had flown the day before from Canada and were about to embark on a two-week mission to build Sunday school rooms for a small Baptist church in a very poor barrio of that city. We had loads of expectations, but I had some lingering yabbuts rattling around in my brain. Would it have been better for us to have just raised the money for this project and stayed comfortably at home? Was this the best way we could live out our yearning to do something special for Jesus?

We had wonderful support back home for this trip, but some questions had been raised. One in particular always seems to pop up when a venture such as this is considered: "There's just so much suffering out there in the world. Do you really think you're going to make any difference? Maybe the mission should begin at home and stay at home."

On that patio the first day, following some singing, the team member whose turn it was to lead the devotion shared a modern parable called the Starfish story. It made such an impression on us that on our second mission to Nicaragua a few years later, we had a starfish printed on our team T-shirts.

The parable developed from a story from scientist and anthropologist Loren Eiseley and has been adapted in many ways. Here's the way I remember the story from that day in Nicaragua.

There was a man who went to the ocean each morning for inspiration for his writing. His habit was to walk along the beach before he began his work. Early one morning, he was walking on the beach after a severe storm had passed through the night, leaving the shore littered with starfish as far as the eye could see.

Off in the distance, the man noticed a small girl approaching. As this child walked, she paused every so often. As they came closer to each other, the man saw that the girl was bending down to pick up an object from the sand. She hurled it out into the sea.

"Good morning," the man called out. "May I ask just what you're doing?"

The girl paused and looked up. "Throwing starfish into the ocean. The high tide after the storm washed them up on the beach, and they can't return to the sea by themselves. They'll die unless I throw them back into the water."

"But there must be thousands of starfish on this beach," the man said. "I'm afraid you won't really be able to make much of a difference."

With that, the girl reached down, picked up yet another starfish, and threw it as far as she could into the ocean. "Well, I made a difference for that one!"

THE GOOD SAMARITAN
READ LUKE 10:22-37

The setting to this parable is interesting. A teacher of the law came to Jesus asking a question that he thought both he and Jesus should know the obvious answer to: "What must I do to receive eternal life?" Jesus directed him to Deuteronomy 6:5 and Leviticus 19:18, which advised people to love God and love their neighbours. So far, so good.

However, this teacher had a further agenda: just how far could a person be expected to go in loving one's neighbour? Jesus replied with this parable, one of the best known of all the stories Jesus told.

A traveller was making his way from Jerusalem to Jericho. This road was infamous for danger. It was seventeen miles in length, descending almost three thousand feet through deep canyons, which afforded great opportunities for robbers and thieves to lie in wait and ambush unwary travellers.

Perhaps at this point the others gathered around the teacher of the law, shaking their heads and thinking, *What foolishness for this traveller to be alone on that treacherous stretch of road.*

And so the traveller was set upon, beaten, robbed, and left for dead. But it appeared that help was in sight, for others were travelling the road that day, too. Two religious officials—a priest and a Levite—showed up. Jericho, like Jerusalem, was a city of priests, so they often travelled back and forth between the two cities. Priests officiated at the Temple and administered all of its rituals and sacrifices. Levites were members of the Jewish tribe of Levi and for generations had served as associates to the priests in the many functions of Temple worship (1 Chronicles 23:24–32).

Neither priest nor Levite stopped to give assistance to the beaten and robbed man lying on the side of the road.

To fully grasp the impact of this parable, consider that those hearing it, and certainly the teacher of the law, would give the two religious officials some benefit of the doubt for not stopping. Both officials would have been very concerned about ritual purity. If the man was dead and they touched him, they would have to undergo a rigorous cleansing, which would have taken them away from their religious responsibilities.

The priest and the Levite practised what could be termed as "the silver rule": do not do to others what you would not have them do for you. Both officials did no harm to the man on the side of the road, but neither did they do him any good.

A third individual appeared on the road, and behold, moved with compassion he stopped and provided assistance to the wounded man, binding his wounds, transporting him to a nearby inn, and paying for his care. Next came the "say what" moment: this compassionate man was a Samaritan.

To understand why this was surprising, we need to consider the level of hatred that existed between Jews and Samaritans of that day.

When the northern kingdom of Israel was conquered by Assyria in 722 BC, thousands of Israel's leading citizens were deported to

Babylon. In time, some of the Israelites still living in the land began to intermarry with the foreigners, creating a mixed race. This was offensive to the Jews who remained pure, so a division developed between Samaritans and Jews that hardened over the years.

When the Jews were rebuilding the Temple in Jerusalem, Samaritans offered their assistance but were refused. The result was that they withdrew from the Jews and built their own Temple on Mount Gerizim.

For the one who stopped to help be a despised Samaritan must have been shocking and offensive to those hearing the story. Jesus, however, wanted to dramatically demonstrate the necessity of linking one's profession of faith to living out that same faith. The Samaritan accomplished this and the two religious officials failed.

The teacher of the law had to admit that the one who truly obeyed the commandment to love his neighbour was the Samaritan. Jesus needed to make the Samaritan's virtue of compassion abundantly clear. Ritual observance, duties, responsibilities, and daily routines meant little to Jesus if they didn't result in action. Helmut Thielicke puts it well:

> We can love only if we have the mind of Jesus and turn the lawyer's question around. Then we shall ask not "who is my neighbour?" but "to whom am I a neighbour?" Who is laid at my door? Who is expecting help from *me* and who looks upon *me* as his neighbour? This reversal of the question is precisely the point of the parable.[13]

THE BEGGAR AND THE RICH MAN
READ LUKE 16:19–31

Another lesson regarding compassion is this rather intriguing story of a rich man and a beggar named Lazarus. Basically, the story describes a man only identified as rich: living in luxury and dressed in the purple and linen of great prosperity. Lazarus, the beggar (Jesus gives a name to this beggar, the only person named in any of the parables), lies at the rich man's gate, covered in sores and longing to eat even the crumbs that might fall from the rich man's table.

---

13 Helmut Thielicke, *The Waiting Father*, 168.

Both men die, and in another great "say what" moment, Jesus creates a reversal. The rich man ends up suffering in hell while Lazarus is taken by the angels to heaven. The rich man is able to gaze up at the scene in heaven. Being parched, he asks for Lazarus to dip his finger in water and come and cool his suffering tongue. This wasn't possible, for a chasm lies between heaven and hell. The rich man then requested that Lazarus be sent to warn his five brothers to avert the same fate. Abraham replies that those brothers, like the rich man himself, have had Moses and the Prophets to warn and teach them. If they hadn't heeded the Scriptures by now, not even someone returning from the dead would influence them.

We need to exercise some caution in interpreting this parable. First of all, let us not write off the rich man too quickly. The problem is not with riches themselves, but rather with not using our material blessings to care for others. As he often did in parables, Jesus was dealing with the Pharisees, who were doing well in Jewish society and were very prosperous. They felt blessed by God through their adherence to the law and rituals of their religion. Indeed, Scripture pointed out that those who obeyed the commands of God would receive blessings (Deuteronomy 28:3–4).

Nor should we glorify Lazarus. Being poor doesn't necessarily make someone more spiritual. Too often, bitterness, depression, and deep suffering characterize the lives of people like Lazarus. We shouldn't blame them for their position, either.

There is a danger in oversimplifying the blessings of God by assuming that those who are rich and prosperous have received God's favour. Along with that is an underlying assumption that those who are poor and needy somehow deserve their fate, that they have put themselves outside the favour of God. That is far too simple and unhelpful, yet the belief seems to persist.

So what is Jesus driving at here?

First of all, the danger for the rich man, and for the Pharisees as well, was to not recognize that all the blessings he enjoyed came from God and provided him a great opportunity to share those blessings. Rather he is only characterized as being rich and indulgent. For me, the key is the fact that for years Lazarus lay at his gate, needy and hungry, and the rich man either ignored or simply didn't even notice him.

Helmut Thielicke points out:

> People whose whole life is absorbed in their wealth have to frolic and regale themselves in order to prevent themselves from seeing that right next door to where they live there is another world, the world of the slums, Lazarus and his filthy rags. So the rich man shuts his eyes whenever his carriage is driven through the slums. He can't bear the thought that this could happen to him *too*. For there would be nothing left of him if he ever had to give up his style of living. He is so utterly hollow that he needs at least this shell of wealth to keep from turning into thin air. He cannot look at Lazarus' sores, otherwise his own well-bathed and perfumed body would begin to itch in its purpose and fine linen. Therefore, keep Lazarus at the back door, so he won't be seen![14]

It would appear that this rich man, like the Pharisees, had celebrated their blessings from God, but they had conveniently forgotten that obligations came with those blessings, according to their Scriptures. The Mosaic Law advocated that at harvest time some produce be left for the poor to gather: *"Do not go back through your vineyards to gather the grapes that were missed or to pick up the grapes that have fallen; leave them for poor people and foreigners"* (Leviticus 19:10). Likewise, along with injunctions for celebrating the seventh or Sabbatical year, the people of Israel were advised, *"There will always be some Israelites who are poor and in need, and so I command you to be generous to them"* (Deuteronomy 15:11).

Lest we miss this point, let me ask this question: how aware are you of those like Lazarus who may lie around your door or live in your neighbourhood? How many suffering people do you pass each day? Does your busyness, preoccupation, schedule, and responsibilities blind you to need? The three individuals who encountered the man who'd been beaten and robbed on the Jericho road were there that day by

14 Ibid., 43.

chance. It is often by chance that God presents us opportunities to live out his compassion each day. How do we act upon those chances?

My wife and I were once delayed at Logan International Airport in Boston as our flight to Toronto was first delayed, then cancelled. As I was about to negotiate seats on a later flight, a woman literally dropped at our feet, feeling very ill. Using my backpack for a pillow, my wife comforted her. However, other people in the lounge simply stepped over her to get to their seats. We discovered that the woman also had been booked on the cancelled flight. Thankfully, we were able to get her a seat on the same flight as us, and upon our arrival in Toronto we waited with her until we knew she had been picked up by someone. It certainly was a chance opportunity to offer the compassion of Jesus!

THE SHEEP AND GOATS
READ MATTHEW 25:31-46

Another striking parable told by Jesus gives us insight into the final judgment that will occur for all humanity. All nations will be gathered before Jesus and be divided into two categories, just like a shepherd will divide his mixed flock of sheep and goats.

On the right hand, the sheep will occupy the place of honour, destined to enter the fullness of God's kingdom. To the left, the goats will be rejected and tormented. What makes the difference? The sheep represent those whose lives have shown evidence of compassion, for Jesus discovers in their acts of loving care that they have actually embraced him. The sheep are surprised, for their acts of compassion weren't calculated for reward but simply given from the heart.

This parable serves as a constant challenge for us to discover the face of Jesus in the outcast, the suffering, and the wounded of our world.

Just as startling are those on the goat side. They had the opportunity to live out compassionate love but failed to reach out to the suffering ones. Jesus was hungry but not fed, naked but not clothed, in prison but ignored. For me, this is a constant challenge as well. I need to discover the face of Jesus in someone who is wounded and suffering, and truly embrace the opportunity to discover and love that person. If I just pass

by and miss the opportunity of care, I court the danger of the goats who
have failed Jesus.

G.A. Studdert-Kennedy captured the danger of passing by Jesus in
a poem set in his home city of Birmingham, England:

When Jesus came to Birmingham, they
simply passed him by;
They never hurt a hair of him,
they only let him die;
For men had grown more tender,
they would not give him pain;
They only passed on down the street,
and left him in the rain.[15]

This echoes the final judgment on the rich man in the first parable.
He had opportunities to live out the commandments found in the Law,
but due to his selfish absorption in his affluence and luxury he failed even
to assist the beggar, whom he must have walked past every day of his life.

We again hear the warning. Do we simply glorify God and worship Jesus in the safe confines of our sanctuaries? Do we occupy ourselves with maintaining those sacred walls at the expense of going out
into the streets to truly meet Jesus?

Let's face it: it isn't easy or comfortable to seek Jesus out on the high-
ways and bi-ways of our world. It gets messy and maybe even dangerous.

Going back to the beginning of this chapter, travelling to Nicaragua
meant a long plane ride and a challenging few weeks in a country far
different from home, yet I eagerly await another trip. I felt that Jesus was
truly present each day of our mission and I received far more than I gave.

Our team received the deep gratitude of the people with whom
we ministered. On our first trip, we built two Sunday school rooms. On
a return visit, the congregation joyfully showed us those rooms filled
with eager children. I can remember the joy with which the staff of a
struggling medical clinic received the supplies we had brought them.

---

15 Neil R. Lightfoot, *Lessons from the Parables* (Grand Rapids, MI: Baker Book House,
1978), 183. Quoting G.A. Studdert-Kennedy.

It was reassuring to make a difference to even one. How, where, and with whom might you make such a difference?

Living Out Our "Say What" Moment

Reflect upon times in your life when someone has truly offered you compassion. What was the circumstance into which they provided help and care? In what way was that compassion expressed? Were you able to truly thank them? If not, can you still express your gratitude? Give God thanks, for indeed, an angel unaware can step into our times of need.

Now reflect upon those times when you extended compassion to others. What was that circumstance? In what way did you express that care and compassion? Consider also the possible times when you have passed by on the other side of the proverbial road. Can you learn from those times when you failed to offer the compassion that was needed?

Let us apply the Starfish principle. Begin to look out for situations where you can make a difference to even one. Remember that the kingdom of God is built person by person, deed by deed. The "mustard seeds" of faith, love, and peace we have the opportunity to plant every day of our lives will bring about an abundant harvest! Don't feel discouraged about not being able to make a huge difference in the hurt and pain of this world. Realize that by offering compassion in one situation to one person, you continue the process of God healing this world.

In reflecting upon the mission trips I've been on, few as they have been, I've been tremendously blessed. I have been strengthened by the faith of brothers and sisters in Jesus who are proclaiming the kingdom in very difficult places, places far more challenging than where I have been privileged to live. Be aware of the rewards that come with being a neighbour.

I am reminded of an old fable I remember hearing years ago. Two monks had been travelling far and wide and now were returning to their monastery high up a mountain. They were both tired but willing to push on to the warmth and light of their home base. However, a storm stirred up when they were halfway up the mountain. The temperature dropped and wind blew snow and ice into their faces. Nevertheless, they trudged on.

Shortly, the monks came upon another traveller on the path who had fallen and couldn't get up. Should they help this stranded person? They only had enough energy left to get to the monastery, so the first monk decided to continue on his journey. The second monk made the choice to stop and help the wounded traveller. With all his remaining strength, the monk hoisted the traveller onto his back and headed upwards.

The storm grew worse, the wind howled, and the snow became even fiercer. Finally, the lights of the monastery were in sight. Just before they reached the door, the first monk was found lying frozen in the snow. The second monk realized that in carrying the injured traveller, he had created just enough extra warmth and strength to make it safely to the monastery. His willingness to help had saved his own life.

A Prayer for Living Out Our "Say What" Moment

Lord God, I am so thankful for the compassion of Jesus. He bore no restrictions to whom he extended his love, healing, forgiveness, and restoration. I am grateful for those times when Jesus has ministered to me. I recognize those individuals whose hands, voices, and prayers have reached out to me in times of need.

Compassionate Jesus, continue to bring me comfort and strength when I am in the dark valleys of life. May I see you, Jesus, in the faces of those to whom I may offer compassion. May I fully realize the abundance with which you have gifted me, and with that the precious opportunities to serve you out of those blessings. Protect me from my own desire for security that would blind me from the needs of those all around me. Give me opportunities to meet you, Jesus, in binding others' wounds and restoring their hope. Jesus, may your people never weary of being your compassion in such a hurting world. In Jesus's name, amen.

One Ear's
Rescue

Appendix

Here's the story I wrote quickly for that little girl mentioned in the introduction.

Once upon a time long ago, three bunnies lived in a deep green forest. You might say they all looked the same, but if you looked closely, each of them had a special appearance. White Paws, of course, had beautiful white fur on her feet which everyone admired. Midnight had the darkest fur you ever saw on a bunny and he was really proud of how he looked.

The third bunny was called One Ear. When she had just been a little bunny, she had been playing with a large group of other rabbits. They were having a wonderful time chasing each other around the open meadow when suddenly a hawk appeared overhead. Every bunny ran in fear. Unfortunately for One Ear, she had become entangled in a huge bramble bush. Part of her left ear was torn away. She was safe, but it hurt really bad.

What hurt more was that the other bunnies often teased her about how she looked. Most of the time she could ignore it, but she felt ashamed of only having one good ear.

One day she was really upset about her missing ear, so she went off into the woods by herself to think. She stayed out too long and it got dark. One Ear was afraid and unsure about how to get back home.

White Paw and Midnight became very worried when One Ear didn't return when the sun went down. They remembered that she had been upset. But where had she gone? They felt that they needed to look for her, but where would they start. Even though it was very dark, they set out to search for One Ear.

After a long time, they still had found no trace of their missing friend. But just when they were about to give up their search, the sky cleared enough to let a big, bright full moon to shine through the clouds. And there, right in front of them, curled up underneath a massive fir tree, was One Ear. They were so happy to have found her and that she was safe.

They all had a big hug together and promised that they would be friends forever and always look after each other. They had come to realize that each of them was special in their own way, even if part of an ear was missing.

About the Author

Ted Creen is a minister of the Presbyterian Church in Canada, now in semi-retirement. After graduating with a M.Div. from Knox College in Toronto, Ted and his wife Lorraine served congregations in Stouffville and Owen Sound, Ontario. Ted is currently the summer pastoral coordinator of Huron Feathers Presbyterian Centre at Sauble Beach, Ontario.

One of Ted's passions in ministry is the teaching/preaching role. Both he and Lorraine are students of the Word and spend much time reading, reflecting, and applying God's truths. This, for Ted, has developed into a writing ministry as well. His first book, *Moving Mountains (or at least managing them)*, used references for mountains through the Scriptures to explore faith today. This book is now out of print.

The creative arts have also played a strong role in Ted's ministry. He has written a number of musical dramas for children based on stories from the Bible. One song from those musicals, *Lead Me, Jesus*, is published in the current Presbyterian hymnbook. For a dramatized worship, Ted memorized Jesus's Sermon on the Mount and recited it in dramatic fashion. It was a profound experience for Ted. He became particularly attracted to the eight beatitudes that begin the Sermon, which led to writing a book, *Get a Life!* This book is currently available through Word Alive Press.

During his time in Owen Sound, Ted became a spiritual advisor to the palliative care team at the local hospital. Along with the medical doctor on the team, Ted has spoken at many venues across Canada. Currently, Ted conducts grief and bereavement support groups. To enable that work, Ted created a special illustrated Christmas story, *Myrrh is Mine*. This book, available through Word Alive Press, offers healing and hope for those dealing with loss at Christmas.

He has received a Doctor of Ministry degree from Princeton Theological Seminary with a thesis based on enabling hope in the terminally ill.

Ted is excited about this new book, *Say What?*, and hopes that it will provide spiritual insights for anyone who reads it. He is always interested in receiving feedback from readers and can be contacted at tedcreen@hotmail.com.